Devotional Stories of Resilience and Positive Thinking

Chicken Soup for the Soul: Devotional Stories of Resilience and Positive Thinking
101 Devotions with Scripture, Real-Life Stories & Custom Prayers
Susan M. Heim and Karen Talcott

Published by Chicken Soup for the Soul, LLC www.chickensoup.com

Front cover image generated using Adobe Firefly from the prompt "Rainbow with clouds."

Interior illustration of dove courtesy of iStockphoto.com (©Oleksandr Slobodianiuk), photo of clouds generated using Adobe Firefly from the prompt "Clouds in blue sky."

Cover and Interior Daniel Zaccari

Distributed to the booktrade by Simon & Schuster. SAN: 200-2442

Publisher's Cataloging-in-Publication Data

Names: Heim, Susan M., editor. | Talcott, Karen, editor.
Title: Chicken soup for the soul : devotional stories of resilience and positive thinking / Susan M. Heim and Karen Talcott
Description: Cos Cob, CT: Chicken Soup for the Soul, LLC, 2024.
Identifiers: LCCN: 2024942045 | ISBN: 978-1-61159-118-7
Subjects: LCSH Christian life--Literary collections. | Christian life--Anecdotes. | Resilience—Anecdotes. | Consolation--Prayers and devotions. | Devotional literature. | BISAC RELIGION / Christian Living / Devotional | RELIGION / Christian Living / Inspirational | RELIGION / Christian Living / Personal Growth
Classification: LCC PN6071.C56 C45 2024 | DDC 810.8/02/0382/48--dc23

PRINTED IN THE UNITED STATES OF AMERICA
on acid∞free paper
30 29 28 27 26 25 24   01 02 03 04 05 06 07 08 09 10

Table of Contents

❶

~Surviving and Thriving~

❷

~Overcoming Loss~

❸
~Mending Relationships~

❹
~Laughter Through Tears~

❺
~Learning from the Little Ones~

❻

~Be Strong and Courageous~

❼

~A Change in Perspective~

8

~Surrendering Our Worries~

9

~Accentuate the Positive~

10

~An Attitude of Gratitude~

⑪

~The Power of Prayer~

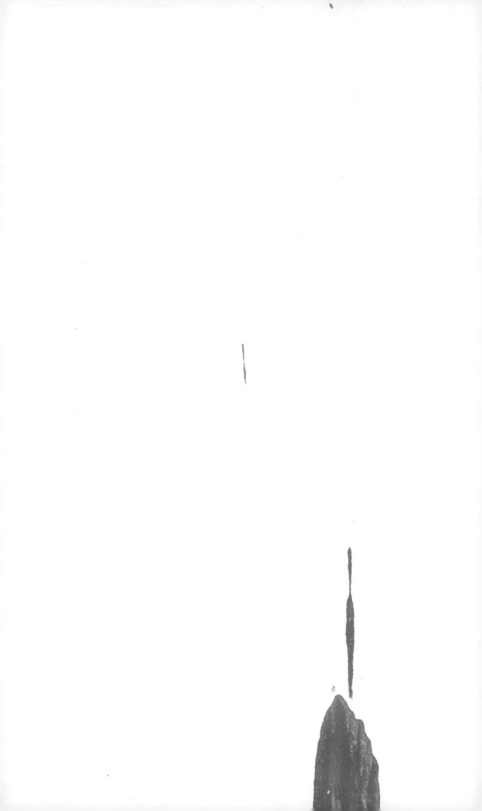

Introduction

I can do all this through him who gives me strength.
~Philippians 4:13

Have you ever felt as if you were riding the roller coaster of life? You may have the option of refusing to ride the roller coaster at the theme park, but none of us can escape the numerous highs and lows that will surely be found on the journey of our lives. It is a ride that we all must take. Fortunately, we can be better prepared for these experiences through our faith in God. He never promised us a life of ease without the inevitable bumps and falls along the way, but he did assure us that he would be with us through it all, the good times and the bad. In Psalm 59:16, we learn of our Father, *"For you are my fortress, my refuge in times of trouble."* Through God's love and support, we can acquire resilience—the ability to come through adversity. This doesn't mean that the difficulties of life will magically disappear, but we can come out of the darkness and into the light with a new appreciation for the lessons we've learned and the strength we've gained.

Trusting God through tough times may provide us with resilience, but we don't need to experience trauma, stress, or fear to practice positive thinking. Think about positive thoughts as preparation for the roller-coaster ride. Positive thinking is the safety belt that makes us feel safer when we're scared or see trouble ahead. When practiced consistently, it puts us in a state of mind where we can better handle the lows and appreciate the highs. When we weave an attitude of gratitude into each day, it gives us strength to tackle whatever comes our way and helps us to focus on the good in our lives. It is choosing to believe that, no matter what is going on today, there are many blessings to be found. In Philippians 4:8, we are told, *"Whatever is true, whatever is noble, whatever is right, whatever is pure, whatever is lovely, whatever is admirable—if anything is excellent or praiseworthy—think about such things."*

This book is filled with true stories written by people just like you who have learned how to accentuate the positive, adopt an attitude of gratitude, surrender their worries, change their perspective, be strong and courageous, and much more. Woven throughout these stories is a message of hope. Hebrews 11:1 tells us, *"Now faith is confidence in what we hope for and assurance about what we do not see."* Sometimes, the clouds obscure our view, and it's hard to see God's hand working in our lives. But these stories show that, when we go through tough times, God is working behind the scenes. With faith and God-given strength, we will weather the storms and find the rainbow on the other side. In fact, a rainbow can't be formed without both sunshine and rain; the combination produces these beautiful arcs of light and signs of hope in our lives.

There are several ways in which you can read *Chicken Soup for the Soul: Devotional Stories of Resilience and Positive Thinking:*

- **Start at the beginning!** Spend a little time with God each day by starting at the beginning of the book and reading a story each day for inspiration.

- **Pray for guidance.** Holding the book closed, pray for God to guide you to just the right devotional that you need to read that day. Randomly open the book and see where the Spirit leads!

- **Select a topic.** If you're dealing with a particular problem, scroll through the table of contents and turn to the appropriate chapter. Select a devotional that applies to your situation.

It is our wish that *Chicken Soup for the Soul: Devotional Stories of Resilience and Positive Thinking* will inspire you, strengthen you, and give you peace in knowing that God walks with you throughout your life. Make prayer and positive thinking a daily practice. You are never alone, for God is with you always. Find comfort in God's promise in Matthew 28:20, *"And surely I am with you always, to the very end of the age."*

—Susan and Karen—

1

When All Doors Close

> *Your ways, God, are holy. What god is as great as*
> *our God? You are the God who performs miracles;*
> *you display your power among the peoples.*
> *~Psalm 77:13-14*

D ead ends. Impossibilities. Closed doors. All applied to me in
my sorry situation.

At age thirty-one, a retinal disease robbed my eyesight
completely. The adjustment was painful. The struggle to navigate
was difficult, and restoring my confidence was slow. But determination
replaced the lack of confidence. I was passionate about caring for my
three-, five- and seven-year-old sons. Groping through each step to
perform household chores, I moved forward.

Sometimes, while at home alone, I fought negative thoughts: What
kind of work does a blind person do anyway? Who would give me a
job? Those were my secret concerns. I hid my feelings of worthlessness
from all those around me.

"Did you ever think of becoming a Spanish interpreter?" a friend
asked me one day.

"No way," I said. "I know nothing about interpreting."

"You speak Spanish," she said, "and that's a good beginning."

I contacted an interpretation company, and they asked me to

come in for an oral test.

The secretary called the next day. "You passed," she said. "In fact, we're going to send you to your first assignment in the Naturalization and Immigration court tomorrow."

I gave a soft gasp. Thrilled and eager to work, I put on my business suit, grabbed my white cane, and held my husband's arm. But while waiting outside the courtroom, doubts ricocheted through my head. I knew nothing about interpretation or court proceedings.

"God, don't let me fall. Guide my steps," I prayed.

With my stomach churning, I began the session by interpreting all I heard in English into Spanish and vice versa.

The judge hit the gavel. "We'll take a ten-minute recess," he said. "Mrs. Eckles, approach the bench."

My hands trembled as I gripped my white cane and headed toward his voice.

"Yes, your Honor," I muttered.

"I'm bilingual," he said, "and I want you to know that I'm impressed with your high level of accuracy and professionalism."

I suppressed a shout of glee and smiled. "Thank you, your Honor."

Soon after, I began an intense study of audio materials on court interpretation. To my delight, I received frequent requests to interpret in civil and criminal courts. Months later, the largest over-the-phone interpreting company in America hired me because of my court experience. Through the years, I received awards for my performance, including the highest and prestigious award of Professional Excellence.

I had viewed myself as worthless; God restored my worth. I saw closed doors; God opened them wide. I lacked the skills, but He provided what I needed. I doubted the outcome, but He showed me the way.

—Janet Perez Eckles—

My Prayer

Father, thank you for seeing beyond my impairment, beyond my limitations, and beyond all of what I thought were impossibilities. I thank you for seeing no one as worthless, blind, deaf or lame. You work wonders through us all!
Amen.

2

My Treasure from God

I was thirty-seven years old when I learned I was expecting my third child. With two older children and working a full-time job, it was difficult to accept this pregnancy.

Because of my age, I scheduled an amniocentesis to check for abnormalities. My doctor agreed but changed his mind just before the test because I had two healthy daughters. I now feel strongly that God was protecting my baby. As I wasn't crazy about being pregnant, I might have considered termination if the test had revealed a birth defect.

Just one hour after delivering my daughter, Melissa, the doctor told my husband and me that our daughter was a "Mongoloid," or mentally retarded. This brought the most agonizing pain my heart had ever gone through. I kept hoping the doctors had misdiagnosed my daughter.

The next day, a social worker showed me brochures of a home for "these kind of children." I told her there was no way I would consider it and demanded she leave my room immediately.

We brought Melissa home, and thus began the lowest times of my life. Her health was not the best, resulting in continuous ER and doctors' visits. I struggled spiritually at first, and just couldn't accept that this was happening to me.

But even though the road was painful, my relationship with the Lord gradually renewed and strengthened. I began to realize that having Melissa, just exactly the way she is, was a gift from God. Her Down's syndrome was not a burden, but a blessing!

Today, Melissa is an adult and the apple of my eye, loved by her entire family. She is happy and in excellent health. She lives a full and productive life, and even has a part-time job at a grocery store. Her room is covered in medals she has won through Special Olympics.

Melissa has accepted Christ into her heart, and knows of Christ's perfect, free gift of forgiveness and eternal love. Many mornings she wakes up and tells me Jesus spoke to her in her dreams. It was a hard road in the beginning, but now Melissa is a treasure from God and my constant companion.

— Clara Riveros —

My Prayer

*Thank you, precious Father, for refining my heart and soul through the trials and tribulations in my life. You know what burdens I can bear and how they can become our greatest blessings.
Help me to trust in that wisdom when I'm going through difficult times.
Amen.*

3

All Things Work Together

And we know that in all things God works
for the good of those who love him, who have
been called according to his purpose.
~Romans 8:28

On December 22, 2008, I arrived to work at my usual time and began my day by reading my e-mails. One e-mail in particular caught my attention. It was from my supervisor, and it read, "I have scheduled a meeting with you at 4:45 P.M. today. If you have already scheduled visits for this time, please reschedule those visits."

All that day I walked around feeling as though I was in limbo. Something just didn't feel quite right. Questions flooded my mind. "Why are my co-workers avoiding me? Why would my supervisor schedule a meeting with me fifteen minutes before the end of the day? Why? Why? Why?"

At the meeting, my supervisor and one of her peers sat across from me as she launched into a discussion regarding my position. Then she casually ended by saying, "And therefore the agency has decided to let you go." As her words echoed in my ears, I felt like a trapeze artist who had flown mid-air and let go of the bars, only to discover that there was no one there to catch me. I imagined myself falling, futilely flailing and screaming, with only three days before Christmas, one work check in my checking account, and six months short of having the ability to obtain the pension that I would have received from the agency as a vested employee.

Despite the media reports of the many unemployed who were losing their homes, I did marvelously the first month of unemployment. I loudly proclaimed that my job was not my god, and just like He blessed me with that job, God would open another door for me. I held on to every scripture in the Bible that spoke of God's faithfulness, chiefly, "… in all things God works for the good of those who love him…"

By the second month of my unemployment, I had run out of money and was two months behind on my rent and car payments. At that point, my fears kicked in and tried to weigh me down with visions of joblessness, homelessness, and no vehicle to escape the winter cold and snow. Many days I held on to God's promises to comfort my distress as I prayed for rescue.

Just as my hopes began to fade, God's faithfulness materialized right before my eyes, and my situation turned around to the good. First, instead of evicting me, my landlord said, "Linda, I'll work with you on this. Just keep me posted as to how things are going." Second, the company that finances my car also agreed to work with me and didn't repossess my car. Finally, I received a call from a temp service that had reviewed my resume online. I ended up being hired for a job where I'm still doing what I love and currently making over $10,000 more per year than I was making at my previous place of employment. God is good.

— Linda A. Haywood —

My Prayer

Dear Father God, thank you for your faithfulness toward us and how you are always working things out on our behalf. Thank you for your presence as we go through every one of our trials and tribulations, and for giving us the reassurance that you indeed are with us always, even unto the end of the world.
Amen.

4

Past My Expiration Date

I lift my eyes to the mountains—where does my help come from? My help comes from the Lord, the Maker of heaven and earth.

~Psalm 121:1-2

I sat with my husband and parents in the bleachers watching my son and daughter march proudly with their teams in the soccer parade. As I raised my arm to wave at them, pain shot from my shoulder to my fingers. A red, stinging rash covered my hand. My head felt as though it would explode at any moment, and I was so dizzy I needed to lie down. Fortunately, the parade came to an end, and I could go home and rest.

I tried to stand, but I couldn't move. Somehow, my family got me down the bleachers and into the car. I was exhausted. As soon as I got home, I fell into bed. After I awoke, I glanced at a mirror. My face was swollen, and a red rash covered the bridge of my nose, part of my cheeks and my forehead.

Two days later, I told the doctor about my experience at the soccer parade. "Shelley," he said gently, "I'm afraid you have lupus." He arranged for me to see a rheumatologist as soon as possible.

I called my husband and mother. Although they were upset, I had an odd sense of peace. For several years, my random symptoms had been severe enough to send me to the doctor. They had tested me for everything, including lupus, but the tests always came back negative. Putting a label on what was wrong with me made it easier. Now my enemy had a name. With God's help, I could fight it.

A few days later, I saw the rheumatologist. This time, my tests came back positive and verified the other doctor's diagnosis. We discussed my treatment and changes I needed to make to my lifestyle. Then he dropped the bomb. He said if I took my medications, got plenty of rest, stayed out of the sun, and got a check-up every three months, I might live as long as ten years… if I was lucky. Ten years sounds like a lot of time, but I had a six-year-old daughter and a nine-year-old son, and it was possible I wouldn't live another year, let alone ten. Even in the best case, I wouldn't be around to see Jessica graduate from high school.

The doctor tried various combinations of medications on me. Some of them made me feel so much sicker that I didn't think I'd make the one-year mark. I joined a lupus support group, but their death rate was high. I dropped out, determined not to join their numbers. As the years went on, I developed more autoimmune problems—fibromyalgia, arthritis, and Sjogren's syndrome—but I kept going.

I asked God for one thing over and over—to let me live long enough to raise my children. He has answered my prayer with abundance. I made it to my ten-year deadline. The years went by. By His grace, I'm fourteen years past what my husband calls "my expiration date."

I will always believe in miracles. After all, I'm living one.

— Shelley Mosley —

My Prayer

Dear Lord, you bless us with your miracles, but too often we don't recognize them for what they are. Help us to see and be thankful for your many gifts. Amen.

5

Kindness with Finesse

A bruised reed he will not break, and a
smoldering wick he will not snuff out,
till he has brought justice through to victory.
~Matthew 12:20

I am grieved to say there was a time in my life when I was living in rebellion against God. I had come to a crisis, and rather than trusting God, my faith utterly failed, and I went the wrong way. This way led downward and finally to homelessness. Unable to find work, I lived in a borrowed car and had little to eat. I was the prodigal in the pigpen. My suffering—all of it deserved—was intense: the gnawing loneliness, the emptiness of my days with nothing to do, the shattering of self-confidence. I even failed at suicide.

One suffocatingly hot summer's evening, feeling emotionally fragile yet desperately homesick for God, I got up the courage to slip into a church service. Acutely aware that I was dirty and inappropriately dressed, I sat in the back. I had planned to sneak out quickly when the service was over so that I wouldn't have to talk to anybody, but the pastor met me at the door.

"How nice to have you visit with us," he said, shaking my hand warmly. "I'm so glad you came."

I could hardly believe that anybody would be so courteous and respectful to someone in my condition. "Thank you," I mumbled, my face flaming.

"What is your situation? Is there anything you need?"

"No, not really." I didn't mean to brush off his question, but I didn't know how to respond to such unexpected concern. I took a step toward the door, but he put his hand on my shoulder.

"Do you have a place to sleep tonight?" he asked quietly.

As embarrassed as I was, I couldn't bring myself to lie to him. "Only my car," I admitted.

I was astonished by what happened next. This kind man gave me a key to the church. He told me to sleep in the church nursery so I could use the air conditioning and to cook in the church kitchen until I could get on my feet. Instead of treating me with disdain, he treated me with dignity and the confidence that I would get on my feet. He gave me hope.

That night as I settled down on a crib mattress on the floor in the cool nursery, I felt assurance that I was still accepted as a child of God. My Heavenly Father was welcoming me home.

Thanks to God and this pastor, I did find a job eventually and got back on my feet—both financially and spiritually.

— Ann McArthur —

My Prayer

Dear God, thank you for extending grace to us, often when we least deserve it. You treat the battered and bruised with such gentleness. Your graciousness is kindness with finesse. Amen.

6

The Golden Summer

You let men ride over our heads;
we went through fire and water, but you
brought us to a place of abundance.
~Psalm 66:12

We lived far below the poverty level, and yet my kids and I luxuriated in the richness of the countryside where we lived. Millions of tiny peepers gave free concerts outside our windows. Beavers added to the rustic music, slapping flat tails against the swampy lake as they worked. Golden eagles and great blue herons soared above. My daughter Sarah coaxed a white swan to eat from her hand that spring.

In spite of my bad marriage, there was much to be thankful for. Riches crammed every lovely nook of our home place. Goldenrod spilled sunshine around like showers of golden treasure. Bejeweled spider webs hovered between blades of grass, heavy with morning dew. Fireflies painted tantalizing patterns against the black velvet darkness, drifting low to the earth to tempt barefooted children with mason jars.

When my husband abandoned us, we were forced to leave our home and rent an apartment in a nearby small town. My grief was unbearable. Not only had I lost the simple dream of raising my children in peace and beauty, but I knew I could never become the father they needed. Since I had to go back to work to support us, I couldn't even be the mother I wanted to be. I thought their childhood was ruined.

I wallowed in self-pity for a while, but one day God showed me a better way. While I couldn't give my kids a good earthly father, I saw that God had promised to be the Father of fatherless children. I asked Him that day to give my children everything that I could not and all that their father would not. I believe the beginning of God's answer to this prayer was "the golden summer," as my kids later named it.

To my children, the summer we moved was one long, happy picnic. For the first time in their lives, they had other kids to play with. Organizing a troop of a dozen or so, they fought "apple wars," a game they invented that involved pelting each other with hard green apples from the overgrown tree in the backyard. This had the added benefit of leaving impressive bruises to show off afterward.

Impromptu wrestling matches flared up in the grass in which my daughter often triumphed over the boys. After a brief summer flood, a neighborhood water-football game sprang up in our yard. One steamy afternoon, a friend's father taught Luke the covert art of hand-fishing in the creek. Evenings were spent practicing marksmanship on our neighbor's unfortunate barn, decorating it with fluorescent pink paintball splats.

The bookmobile trundled into town every other Saturday carrying friendly traveling librarians who offered delicious books to be devoured on rainy days. Secrets were whispered as young companions stargazed from the shelter of the tree house. The Fourth of July arrived, and we trooped toward the park, hauling blankets for spreading on the grass. The fireworks were especially fine that year, improved further by the rare treats of cotton candy and freshly pulled taffy.

These are the things my children remember about "the golden summer," not the things they lost. In their minds, its greatness will never be equaled.

Sometimes, I forget that God answers prayers in His own creative way, and rarely in a manner that I expect. My children played carefree that summer, forgetting the unpleasant parts of life with their earthly father. They were safe and cared for then, as they are now. A mother needn't worry when God puts His hand to the task of fathering.

— Rhonda Brunea —

My Prayer

Dear God, what a rich and wonderful world we are blessed to live in! Thank you for being our Creator and our Heavenly Father, who is the perfect parent for our children.
Amen.

7

For Everything There Is a Season

But those who hope in the LORD will renew their strength. They will soar on wings like eagles; they will run and not grow weary, they will walk and not be faint.

~Isaiah 40:31

Our daughter was diagnosed with a rare tumor in her hip socket. She had two major hip surgeries and spent months in therapy and a wheelchair, followed by crutches. Six months after the second surgery, we lost our barn and dairy operation in a ferocious fire. We watched in devastation as a part of history and our lives burned to the ground.

Five months later, during the clean-up and reconstruction of the barns, my husband had his right leg amputated due to a serious farm accident. While dealing with this difficult situation, I severely burnt my right hand. I was afraid of how this would affect my ability to play the piano, my life's passion. Due to overuse of my left hand, I had carpal tunnel surgery. Things started to get back to "almost" normal when certain events and difficult situations caused our family to leave our home church.

I felt like I had lost everything. I had to hold on to God's promises. Even though I knew God was there and would not leave me—that He has a reason for everything—I still had moments when I cried out to Him, "Why?"

But by trusting in God, our family gained wisdom from the difficulties we experienced. Our barn and dairy were rebuilt with the help of friends and family. My husband continued farming and inspired other amputees by sharing his experience. We joined a larger church where I became the drama director and keyboardist in the Faith Praise Ensemble. Our daughter's experience led her to finish her master's degree as a radiologist assistant.

When our faith is tested, it teaches endurance and equips us with strength for tomorrow. God specializes in using our trials to prepare us to accomplish the awesome!

— Sandra Diane Stout —

My Prayer

Heavenly Father, you are a great God. As I meet today's trials and frustrations, give me renewed awareness of your constant, loving presence. May I not forget that I am here to serve you. May I use the wisdom and strength I gain from my trials to bring your love to those around me.
Amen.

8

Anna Mary's Advice

"For where two or three gather in my name,
there am I with them."
~Matthew 18:20

S urprise tinged with a hint of alarm showed on my face at the
doctor's words: "You're pregnant!" My husband and I had
recently relocated, so when Dick and I heard we were having
a baby, we felt understandably overwhelmed!

"We don't really know anyone here yet," I fretted in a phone call
to my mother-in-law, Anna Mary. "With no family nearby, who will
help us with the baby?"

"You will do just fine," Anna Mary assured me. After a pause, she
asked, "Do you remember Harry Sagar, the Methodist pastor?"

"Yes. Nice, quiet guy, right?" I recalled the minister who seemed
to exude a calming strength.

"Yes! Harry was so helpful when our church didn't have a pastor,
and our family went through a rough patch," she shared. "Did you
know he moved to a church near where you and Dick are living?"

"No, I hadn't heard that," I answered, my curiosity piqued.

"You've always been involved in the church. Maybe you could give
Harry's church a try. I can find the name of it if you want," she offered.

Her simple, God-inspired suggestion turned out to be the best parenting advice Dick and I ever received.

The church was just a mile from our apartment. Though only passing acquaintances with Pastor Sagar, it was nice to see a familiar face when we entered the sanctuary.

Harry introduced us around, and we bonded immediately with the warm, welcoming congregation. One family in particular, the Armels, gathered Dick and me under their wing and treated us like family. In the ensuing months, Lucy, the mother, often invited us to their home.

When I experienced some discomfort close to my due date, we drove to the Armel home to check things out with Lucy. About two hours later, she said, "Pam, I've been watching your face and my watch. You're in labor. I think it's time you headed for the hospital."

Our son was born seven hours later!

Over the years and moves that followed, Anna Mary's advice repeatedly proved to be a blessing from God. Fostered by the wonderful people in the congregation, our children never lacked a grandmotherly hug or a doting babysitter. Like a surrogate family, experienced parents and caring fellow believers became a sounding board for our many questions and gave us the opportunity for some adult conversation.

However, the greatest benefit of involving ourselves in the church was the opportunity to grow spiritually—to cultivate a relationship with God, who then equipped Dick and me to be better partners and parents.

Our children now have kids of their own. They, too, live far from family. Knowing firsthand the parenting challenges they face, I have shared with them the wise counsel that Anna Mary gave me: Find a welcoming church and get involved! There God will provide all the support and encouragement you will ever need.

—Pam Williams—

My Prayer

Lord, you know we can't carry the responsibilities of parenting alone. Please lead us to a caring faith community where we can grow in our relationship with you as well as uphold one another.
Amen.

9

A Harvest of Blessing

Even now the one who reaps draws a wage and harvests a crop for eternal life, so that the sower and the reaper may be glad together.
~John 4:36

As a young bride, I had no idea what older women meant when they said marriage was hard work. "Hard work?" I asked, somewhat surprised. I was blissfully married to my best friend, my college sweetheart. We were having too much fun forging our new life together to consider it work, much less hard. We both had good jobs with comfortable salaries that allowed us to purchase two new vehicles, take weekend trips, and basically enjoy life. A year after our wedding, we bought our first house. Three years later, we brought our first son home, followed two years later by his brother. Life was very full.

That's when the hard work of marriage slapped me in the face.

Consumed with being a good mother, I didn't realize I'd stopped being a good wife. Raising well-adjusted, happy kids became my priority. Because I'd quit my job to stay home with the boys, finances were tight. Stresses we hadn't experienced in our early years of marriage began to chip away at our relationship.

With my husband working long hours, and me filling my days with the boys' school, church and sports activities, plus my own activities and ministries that kept me busy, it was shocking to one day discover how far apart my husband and I had grown. I clearly recall telling a friend that I felt like Brian and I were roommates instead of husband and wife. How had this happened?

Looking back, I see how I let everything and everyone take precedence over Brian and our marriage. I didn't mean to do it nor did I even recognize that it was happening. But after eighteen years of marriage, we'd reached a place where we had to make a decision: Work on our marriage and move forward, or quit.

During those painful months, God made something very clear to me. He'd given me the desire of my heart, which was to be married to my best friend. Brian was my first priority. Being a wife was my most important ministry. I could not continue to put our two precious children ahead of my husband all the time.

With God's help, we made it through those turbulent waters. It took both of us making changes. We had to learn to love and respect each other all over again. This year, we'll celebrate twenty-six years of marriage. And I can honestly say our marriage is healthier and happier than it has ever been. We didn't give up when things got tough, and now we are reaping a harvest of blessing.

— Michelle Shocklee —

My Prayer

Lord, when things get difficult in my life, teach me to recognize and realign my priorities. May I recall your promise to give us a harvest if we don't give up.
Amen.

10

The Darkness in My Heart

"You have heard that it was said to the people long ago, 'You shall not murder, and anyone who murders will be subject to judgment.' But I tell you that anyone who is angry with a brother or sister will be subject to judgment..."
~Matthew 5:21-22

I had a right to be angry, and I knew it. Already, I had lived a couple of years without my brother while the man who had killed him walked free.

I remember seeing that man the night of the crash. He seemed to care little that he had driven drunk, causing the crash. A year later during the civil trial, his attorney tried to make it look like it was all my brother's fault. My brother had too much to drink, too, he said. The headlight on his motorcycle was not functioning, he said. Lab tests refuted those claims. The whole time, that man said little.

I wanted him to be sorry. I wanted him to say he was sorry. I didn't get what I wanted. And my anger simmered and grew and boiled and threatened.

He continued with his life. My family tried to continue without my brother.

As time passed, I found myself wishing bad things on that man. Maybe something bad would happen to him. When nothing bad happened, my frustration grew. Didn't he deserve it? Where was God? Was there no justice?

Then one dark night, I imagined myself getting my revenge.

It didn't bring me comfort. Instead, it brought me terror. Was I actually capable of such dark thoughts and disturbing wishes? I was shocked at how dark my mind had become, and more shocked at how it had colored my whole life. My anger revealed itself in my attitudes and actions, coloring my dreams and my whole life in ever-darkening shades.

I can't remember how it came about, but somehow God made His Word known in my mind. I heard Jesus's words that I would be subject to judgment, and I saw with sudden clarity how guilty I was. I had allowed my heart to wander so far that I had actually wished death on that man, and I cared little that I felt that way. I wasn't sorry.

With equal clarity, I suddenly saw that the forgiveness Christ wanted me to extend to the man was not for his sake, but for my own. My anger wasn't hurting him; it was only hurting me. Forgiving him was not letting him off the hook for what he had done. Forgiving him meant my own anger would not eat me alive from the inside out.

In the decades since, I've actually found myself praying for that man. I don't know where he is now or what he has done with his life since then, but my hope is that God somehow made His Word known to him, and that he has come to know the Savior. If the Lord ever causes our paths to cross again, I'd like to be able to tell him about Jesus, and that His forgiveness of my sins has made all the difference in my life.

— Dianne E. Butts —

My Prayer

Father, when we are angry at someone because of their sin, remind us that our own sins are just as big in your sight. Help us understand that if we refuse to forgive others, we really haven't grasped how much you have forgiven us for our own mistakes. You are the only way that leads to life eternal.
Amen.

11

Here's to You, Grandpa!

The Levites calmed all the people, saying, "Be still, for this is a holy day. Do not grieve." Then all the people went away to eat and drink, to send portions of food and to celebrate with great joy, because they now understood the words that had been made known to them.
~Nehemiah 8:11-12

My father-in-law passed away from lung cancer. At ninety-two, Mom could no longer live alone, so she came to live with us. We managed to get through the sad weeks and months ahead by getting used to each other and the new living arrangements.

Still, we seldom spotted a smile on Mom's face.

Then our married daughters and their families paid us a visit. We got together one evening at a favorite restaurant we'd often frequented when Dad was still with us. I wondered if it would make Mom even sadder.

"It would probably be best not to bring up old memories," I thought to myself as we pulled into the parking lot.

After we'd gotten situated around a large oval table, our younger daughter raised her glass of iced water into the air.

"Here's to Grandpa, and the way he'd always ask to see the chef after a delicious meal," she toasted, clinking glasses with her husband, Greg.

"Remember the time he tried speaking in Italian to the waiter?" our older daughter piped up. "He ordered some strange dessert called 'baldino.' The poor waiter thought he was referring to his bald head."

I glanced across the table in time to see a smile creeping across Mom's wrinkled face.

"Remember the time he sneezed so loudly at the mall that it echoed across the food court? The entire room grew silent!"

"What about the time he couldn't hear the announcer's warning about a tornado alert and asked everyone why there was a TOMATO alert?"

Mom suddenly chuckled.

As I watched everyone wiping happy tears from their cheeks with linen napkins, I relaxed for the first time all evening.

Our food arrived. We continued reminiscing and sharing happy memories of a precious family member who would live on in our hearts forever.

I learned an important lesson from our youngest family member that evening. Sharing memories of a loved one can be a healing thing… a good thing even.

How would Dad have said it?

È una buona cosa! A good thing indeed…

— Mary Z. Whitney —

My Prayer

Father, if we raise our children to be godly, they will teach us about your loving kindness at times when we least expect it. Thank you for family and for our love for each other.
Amen.

12

Angels Among Us

So do not fear, for I am with you; do not be dismayed,
for I am your God. I will strengthen you and help you;
I will uphold you with my righteous right hand.
~Isaiah 41:10

I t was one o'clock in the morning when the call came, but I had already known for hours that he was gone. A mother knows when something has happened to her child. She feels it instinctively, in her bones. But as much as I didn't want to believe it, as much as I had been trying to convince myself that there was a logical explanation for why I wasn't able to reach my son, the police confirmed my worst nightmare.

I had to go to the impound lot to claim his car and empty it. It was the hardest thing I ever had to do. At first, I told myself I never wanted to see that car again. But after eight weeks, I needed to see and touch anything that belonged to him.

I started sobbing the moment his car came into view. Even from a distance, I could see the white sheet crumpled up on the seat, the exact place where my son had died. The lady who worked there must have seen my face and thought I might pass out because a second later she was by my side. She walked with me over to the car, and the first thing I saw were his sandals on the floor. They were left sitting up, as if he had just slipped his feet out of them. I reached down and grabbed them, feeling as though I was taking my son out of the car myself. I held the shoes close to my chest, and I felt the woman's arms around me, embracing me as my heart broke.

"I have a son, too," she said. "Lean on me."

That woman stayed with me, holding me up the entire time as I emptied the car. Her presence and her voice calmed me. Every time my knees grew a little wobbly, she'd whisper those three words again, "Lean on me."

I never got the woman's name, nor do I remember her face. All I remember is the compassion I saw in her eyes. I believe God sends people into our lives, instruments of His peace. And, in that moment, they act as angels, holding us up when we need them the most.

— Darlene Hierholzer —

My Prayer

Sometimes in our lives we need to lean on others to make it through a difficult time. I thank you, Lord, that you send these sweet souls to us. They often show up without being called, but they help make our trials so much easier to bear. Amen.

13

The Child Who Never Came

My comfort in my suffering is this:
Your promise preserves my life.
~Psalm 119:50

After just two months of "trying," I got great news: I was pregnant! I was absolutely thrilled. But because I knew that the first three months of pregnancy could be delicate, I told only my closest family members and my boss. I experienced a little morning sickness, but it stopped around seven weeks. I was so lucky! Everything was going beautifully. At the end of my twelfth week, I decided it was time to share the news at work. We were having a staff meeting, so I chose that time to make the announcement. Everyone was delighted for me. After I left the meeting, I went into the ladies' room. There I discovered a heartbreaking sight: blood. I was losing the baby.

An ultrasound revealed that the baby had only developed to seven weeks—the very same time when my morning sickness went away. I was devastated. Not surprisingly, I struggled with the reasons for my miscarriage. I hadn't touched a drop of alcohol or caffeine. I'd taken my prenatal vitamins and avoided pesticides and harsh cleaning products.

I'd taken such good care of myself and my baby. But the child wasn't meant to be, and I couldn't understand why God had let this happen.

Meanwhile, my co-workers gathered around me. I discovered that four out of the five women with whom I worked directly had miscarried at one point. All four had gone on to have successful pregnancies. The fifth woman struggled with infertility but later happily adopted. These women understood the pain I felt at losing my child, and were able to comfort me during the times when I just wanted to curl up under the covers and not face the world.

I will never know why my first baby died, but I thank God for surrounding me with friends who knew exactly how I was feeling. With no family around, my co-workers became a safe port during a very rocky time in my life. I felt God's presence through their kind words and actions. They carried my burden when I feared I could no longer do so. And I will be forever grateful for the strength of their arms, which could only have come from our Father.

—Susan M. Heim—

My Prayer

Dear God, give us the courage to share our sorrows when they threaten to overwhelm us. Please bring people into our lives who can share the tremendous love you freely give to us all. May we recognize your presence in the faces of those around us.
Amen.

14

Signs of David

Even though I walk through the valley of the shadow of death, I will fear no evil, for you are with me; your rod and your staff, they comfort me.

~Psalm 23:4

I was dyeing Easter eggs with my children when I got the call on March 22, 2008. "Laurie, this is Brad. There's no easy way to say this, but Stacy's dead. She shot herself today…"

Wa-wa, wa-wa, wa-wa. The words sounded as muffled as the teacher's voice in *Peanuts*. My heart became a trombone. I went numb. How could my best friend be gone?

After Stacy's death, there was a void in my life. We had spent almost every day together while our kids were in school. I found it difficult to eat and perform my daily duties as wife and mother. I was depressed.

Several Saturdays later, I drove over to my church and sat outside in front of the statue of the Virgin Mary. Spring flowers decorated the grounds, but all I saw was gray.

"Dear God, please give me a sign that Stacy's all right. I need to know she is with you. Help me get through this difficult time," I cried.

Suddenly, a cool breeze gently fanned my teary face. It was not a windy day. I felt compelled to go inside the church and pray. After kneeling for several minutes, I had an intuitive thought to walk over to the priest's confessional room. Surprisingly, the door was open.

I sat down in front of the welcoming priest and began to sob uncontrollably. I told him the story of Stacy's death, her heartache, and our unique friendship.

"God must have sent me here to talk to you. I feel so much better now," I said.

The priest took my hands and leaned closer to me.

"I feel the presence of a spiritual being from a different plane in this room today."

He paused. I glanced up and noticed his eyes were closed.

"Stacy needs your prayers. Whenever you are sad, pray for her. Remember the conversations and special times you shared. She will live on in your heart and memories."

I could still help Stacy through prayer? I felt like a swaddled newborn being comforted by my father. Hope filled the hole in my heart.

Later that night, as I thought about my visit with the priest, I remembered a conversation Stacy and I once had about the name "David." Everyone named David in her life was special—her father, brother, a mutual friend. They reminded her of David from the Bible, forever seeking God's will.

A tingling sensation flowed through my body. It was as if a current of electricity spread peace within. The priest I had spoken with that day was named Father David! I knew it was no coincidence. God had sent me into the church so that Father David could comfort me. I asked, and He answered. I bowed my head in gratitude.

—Laurie Kolp—

My Prayer

God, thank you for sending me signs that I am not alone.
Help me to recognize these extraordinary "God-incidences"
in my life, thus allowing my aching heart to heal.
Amen.

15

Broken Dishes, Healing Hearts

"... Each of you is to take up a stone on his shoulder, according to the number of the tribes of the Israelites, to serve as a sign among you. In the future, when your children ask you, 'What do these stones mean?' tell them..."
~Joshua 4:5-7

For months, my husband Erik had been battling cancer. Nearing the end of his treatment, his pain had grown increasingly worse. Every movement caused excruciating pain, and noises—even happy ones—over-stimulated him. I was on constant guard to keep the kids quiet, but it was becoming an unreasonable expectation.

One specific night seemed worse than most. Parker, our nine-year-old son, had been badgering and irritating his eleven-year-old sister, eventually provoking her to act upon her redheaded temperament. I had interrupted and shushed arguments all night long when I finally blew my top. I didn't realize how much frustration was pent up inside of my son because he threw the mother of all temper tantrums. In horror,

I watched as he threw himself to the floor, thrashing and screaming. I was very close to joining him in his meltdown when I heard God's quiet voice saying, "Let him break something. He's angry." Then the image of my kitchen dishes came to mind.

I ran to the kitchen and gathered as many plates, cups, and bowls as I could carry and went downstairs. With my arms full, I told Parker to follow me. With an angry sigh, he followed, probably expecting to be punished for his outburst. Instead, I handed him a plate, pointed at the wall, and said, "Throw it." He looked at me, raising his eyebrow, so I grabbed a cup and threw it against the wall. This time, he looked at me like I had lost my mind.

"Throw the plate," I repeated. With a tentative look and a sissy throw, he tossed it, not even breaking it. So I said, "Pick it up and really throw it. Smash it like you mean it." I picked up another dish and threw it. "I hate you, cancer!" I yelled.

Finally understanding what I was doing, Parker picked up the dish and chucked it hard. "I hate Dad being sick!" he yelled, smashing a plate against the wall. "You suck, cancer!" Another dish shattered. "I want my dad back." More shards of dishes littered the floor. And, finally, he shouted, "I don't want my dad to die!" He dissolved into tears.

Reaching the end of our rampage, we sat on the floor in the midst of all the pieces and cried. Relief flooded our hearts. The pressure valve released.

We ate from paper plates for a while. Our friends and family thought I was crazy for destroying every dish in my kitchen. I realize they only saw the "value" of my dishes, but that night was one that neither Parker nor I will ever forget. It was when he realized that I valued his emotions and wellbeing over any material thing in my house.

Shortly after this took place, I read Joshua 4:5-7: "Each of you is to take up a stone on his shoulder… to serve as a sign among you. In the future, when your children ask you, 'What do these stones mean?' tell them…." It sparked an idea.

A few months later, when Erik finished treatment and got back on his feet, Parker and I created a set of mosaic stepping stones from the broken dishes. And someday, when he has a home of his own, I will give him one so he will always have a reminder of the healing that took place that night.

—Jennie Bradstreet Hall—

My Prayer

Lord, many times our children suffer when bad things happen to us here on Earth. Guide and protect them in every moment of every day so that they may know you are near. In your loving name… Amen.

16

God's Great Bear Hug

Get rid of all bitterness, rage and anger, brawling
and slander, along with every form of malice.
Be kind and compassionate to one another, forgiving
each other, just as in Christ God forgave you.
~Ephesians 4:31-32

"God, how could you be so cruel?" I yelled into the air. "Do you really care about me or is this religion stuff all just a hoax?"

I waited for an answer, a sign that God had heard me and was there to comfort me. But the only thing I felt around me was my pain and heartache. The funeral for my mother was still too fresh in my mind to ponder.

Sitting alone in my apartment, my mind replayed the past few years. First, my father had been stricken with cancer. He fought a valiant fight, but he only survived eight months after his diagnosis. Soon afterward, my mother received the news that her breast cancer had recurred. She too didn't take this dreaded disease lying down, but the end results were the same. The two people I needed, cherished, and loved most in the world were suddenly stripped from my life, and I was left alone. It seemed cruel, and I wasn't afraid to rage at

God for my loss.

I sat there for a long time in the darkness. Nothing in my life made sense anymore. Over time, the anger slowly seeped out of me, but numbness took its place. I decided that I didn't want to be in a relationship with God. I stopped all my church activities and found things to do on Sunday mornings. I slept in, read the paper, and even went to breakfast. Filling my life with these activities dampened the pain, and I thought life was slowly returning to normal.

But, to my surprise, I woke one Sunday morning with a feeling of unease. Pacing around my apartment, an inner battle began to rage. Did I want to keep living my life like this or was it time to return to God? Still without a clear heavenly answer, I decided to attend the morning church service. I was now running late, which suited me fine as I slipped into the back row unnoticed. As I sat through the service, my heart began to thaw just a little. It wasn't a huge, noticeable shift, but for the first time in many months I didn't feel so angry.

Returning to my apartment, my heart and mind were at war. I was torn between holding onto my grudge with God or letting it go and starting fresh.

"God, can you take on a battered Christian?" I asked. "Do you really want me back after I blamed you for the deaths of my parents?"

There was silence for a moment, but then almost like a movie was being played out in my head, I saw a father throw everything aside as he ran toward his wayward son. He pulled him into a tight bear hug, and they stood embracing for a long time. The father whispered something into his son's ear, and a deep look of understanding passed between them.

The scene disappeared from my vision, but I knew this prodigal son message was heaven-sent. My bitterness was forgiven, and my true Father was welcoming me back. So I did the only thing I knew how—I put my arms around my Father and simply hugged Him back.

—Karen Talcott —

My Prayer

Dear Heavenly Father, how I must test your patience and love for me. Forgive me when I blame you for the unfortunate events in my life. I thank you for your deep, abiding love that always welcomes me back.

Amen.

17

For Better or for Worse

For you have been my refuge, a strong tower against the foe. I long to dwell in your tent forever and take refuge in the shelter of your wings.
~Psalm 61:3-4

Taking walks around the campus of the university we attended, my husband-to-be and I often talked of all the things life would hold for us as a married couple. Rainy days were among our favorite times to walk, sharing an umbrella and a sense of closeness in the not-so-pleasant weather. Little did we know just how significant the happy memories of rainy day walks would become as we were called to weather a marriage filled with as many rainy days as sunny ones.

I never dreamed I would watch my husband carry the coffin of our infant daughter Adrienne to a hearse after her death from SIDS in 1992. I never thought that my husband and I would spend more than three years of our marriage traveling back and forth to different oncology offices, surgeries, and chemo treatments with our son who was battling brain cancer, and that this journey with our thirteen-year-old son would end with me listening to my husband speak at Nick's funeral.

When two people decide to live the rest of their lives together "for better or for worse," they usually aren't picturing all of the "for worse" moments that can happen along the way. I know I didn't envision this kind of future as I walked down the aisle to say "I do" to Tim. According to *Jane Brody's Guide to the Great Beyond*, "One-fourth to one-third of parents who lose a child report that their marriage suffers strains that sometimes prove irreparable."

As I reflect on how our marriage has survived such trauma, my mind wanders back to our days of walking under an umbrella together. I believe God planned those moments long ago to teach me a lesson I would not fully grasp until today.

Looking back, I realize that we were able to enjoy those rainy day walks in college because we walked with protection over our heads, we held each other's hand, and we knew that sunny days would follow. Today, in our grief, we share those same figurative truths in our rainy seasons of marriage. God is our shelter overhead in times of storms, we hold onto each other in our sadness, and we know and believe that because God's Son conquered death on the cross, our daughter and son experience a sunny eternity with Him today.

I am thankful today, even though my heart is broken, because the God of rainy days and sunny days leads me and my husband as we walk through this life together… for better or for worse.

— Tammy A. Nischan —

My Prayer

Heavenly Father, thank you for being our everlasting source of strength during our trials and tribulations. Even when our hearts are broken, you provide a hope that tomorrow will be better. You are with me and my loved ones, always.
Amen.

18

Faithful Friends

If one falls down, his friend can help him up.
But pity the man who falls and has no one
to help him up.
~Ecclesiastes 4:10

When my friend, Dawn, lost her twenty-one-year-old son, Jason, in an Air Force helicopter crash in Afghanistan, her husband (her son's stepfather) and her daughters were very supportive, but they were going through their own grieving process. It was Dawn's female friends who really got her through that horrendous first year.

Her local friends called all of her out-of-state friends to break the sad news. They made sure that Dawn ate and slept and continued to care for herself. They looked after her teenage daughters, cooked numerous dinners for the family, and cleaned the house. Even after the funeral services, they continued to be there for Dawn in whatever way possible. Dawn doesn't think she would have survived her grief that first year without her friends.

And today, many years later, Dawn's friends are still coming through for her. Dawn established a scholarship fund in her son's name for students at his former high school. His passions were swimming and art, so every year Dawn and her friends hold a beautiful banquet to honor Jason and award scholarships to deserving swimmers and artists. Again, Dawn knows that she could never put this event together alone. Each year without fail, her friends are there to help with mailing invitations, lining up speakers, assessing applications, fundraising, and more.

Faithful friends make the good times better and the bad times more bearable. They are representatives of God's love and compassion during our earthly lives. Lean on your friends during times of trouble and let them bless you with their time and their love.

—Susan M. Heim—

My Prayer

Heavenly Father, I am so very grateful for the friends in my life. Thank you for sending them to me when I need them most. Help me to be as good a friend to them as they are to me.
Amen.

19

Mending a Friendship

Get rid of the old yeast that you may be a new batch
without yeast—as you really are... Therefore let us
keep the Festival, not with the old yeast, the yeast of
malice and wickedness, but with bread without yeast,
the bread of sincerity and truth.
~1 Corinthians 5:7-8

When I first moved to Florida, I felt so out of place. I had come from a small town out West and was so unsure of myself. Luckily, my husband and I moved into a friendly neighborhood, and things became instantly better.

For many years, my neighbor across the street and I shared happy times. But then a misunderstanding developed, and she quit speaking to me. I tried many times to speak to her about the issue and tell her how sorry I was that I had let her down. But she refused to take my phone calls and avoided me when I was outside.

During our stalemate, my husband and I put our house up for sale. We weren't leaving the neighborhood out of spite; we were having twins and needed room for our growing family.

Months later, I moved away without talking to her and putting closure to our misunderstanding. It always left a raw place in my heart when I thought of how poorly it had ended. Many times in church when I prayed, I would flash back to this friendship. Sometimes, I would feel anger still lurking in my heart. Other times, I wanted to find peace again. I just hated the feelings left from our unresolved dispute. It was like a scab that kept reopening and festering with pain and frustration.

About eight months after we moved, I decided to take a drive back into the old neighborhood. As I drove down my street, I saw my former neighbor out in her front yard washing her car. I knew that I needed to stop and greet her. I opened up the car door and got out. To my surprise, she came up and gave me a big hug. We both apologized for our actions, and I felt that closure had finally occurred. I was able to say I was sorry and have it accepted. I know that God heard my prayers and arranged for us to meet that day.

— Karen Talcott —

My Prayer

Dearest Father, please help me to cleanse and purify my old relationships. Enable me to put to rest the relationships that no longer serve my best life, while opening the door for new and lasting friendships.
Amen.

20

Sweet Rest

*"Come to me, all you who are weary and burdened,
and I will give you rest."*
~Matthew 11:28

I n times of turmoil and great personal anguish, I used to find it difficult to sleep. In the deep of night, my mind would scramble from the very present troubles going on in my life to nightmarish visions of possible outcomes, the peace-stealing "what-ifs."

I remember a particular season of my life when the nighttime threatened to devour me. Our nineteen-year-old daughter had moved six-and-a-half hours away, determined to live her life the way she thought suitable. Her idea of suitable and ours were as distant as the miles between us. She wouldn't listen, and her father and I could not acquiesce. Our relationship with our daughter was on the verge of fracturing.

During the day, I battled despair by praying and keeping busy. In the silence of the night, however, I was bedeviled by negative, consuming thoughts. My mind became a battleground, a place where I waged war with my daughter's rebellion. Yet even in my imagination, I was unable to construct a happy ending.

Then, one day, I recognized that I had to quit trying to control the situation and completely release my daughter into God's hands. I finally came to terms with the fact that my struggle to control things was futile. Her father and I had done everything we could; we had said everything that could possibly be said, and none of it was working. I couldn't wage war with my daughter or with myself anymore. I opened the palms of my hands toward the sky and released my precious girl's life, her future, to God. It was then that my wrestling finally ceased.

I decided from then on that I would thank God for what He had in store for us and our daughter, regardless of the pain we were feeling or the outcome. And, oddly enough, in the midst of it all, I was able to see some of my own rebellion and ungodly attitudes. My eyes had been opened. Where I had once prayed for God to change my daughter, I began to pray for Him to change me instead.

It is by God's grace and His grace alone that our daughter found her way back. Because of His work in our lives, our relationship has not only been restored, but it is beautiful and authentic in a way it was not before. We know, however, that things do not always work out that way.

When trouble comes—and it has and will again—I remember the time I lifted my palms to God on behalf of my daughter, and I lift them up anew. I pray and ask God to guide and change my heart and attitudes where I err. I hand over my troubles and my feeble attempts to fix things. It is in this place of prayer that my burdens and troubles move from my open palms to the shoulders of a loving God more than capable of handling every situation.

And it is there I find sweet rest.

— Mary Hughes —

My Prayer

Lord, when life's troubles come my way, I will
lift my eyes and my palms to you. I trust you
completely with my burdens and their outcomes.
In you, I find my rest.
Amen.

21

The Compromise

*The LORD gives strength to his people; the LORD
blesses his people with peace.*
~Psalm 29:11

During the early years of our marriage, my husband and I often disagreed about money. Our priorities were worlds apart, and sometimes it seemed that we would never come to an agreement. Although our combined salaries were enough to get by, we never seemed to have enough money for extras, like making improvements to the fixer-upper home we lived in.

One year, we were excited to learn we would receive a sizable tax refund… and then the debate began. My husband wanted to build a large shed in the back yard to hold the lawn mower, tools and other things that cluttered our garage. As for me, I dreamed of having a nice front porch with rails all around and a swing. I imagined many hours of relaxation and enjoyment for us, our families, and our friends. It was a matter of need versus want. We had many discussions.

Each of our discussions began nicely enough. We calmly shared our ideas and stated the pros and cons for each. Still, our "discussions" repeatedly turned into heated arguments with no apparent solutions.

One Sunday morning while attending church services, I realized suddenly that I had not prayed about this problem. This tax refund was such a blessing to my family, and I had not even been thankful for it. I had been so busy trying to justify my reasons for wanting a porch, and arguing with my husband, that I had neglected to ask God for guidance.

That morning, I gave the problem to the Lord and prayed that peace would be restored to my home. I asked that I would be strong enough to accept the outcome of this dilemma, even if it did not go my way.

A few months later, we began building a shed out in our back yard. Yes, my husband got his shed. I was at peace with that, especially when he began adding a porch to it, complete with rails and a swing.

My "front" porch was actually in the back yard, although it turned out to be the perfect spot. It was near the garden and was a shady place to rest and enjoy a cool drink with my girls on hot summer days. I often sat in the swing watching them play as I shelled beans and peas. Many evenings, we also shared this spot with our neighbors as we chatted and supervised our children while they spent time together.

My husband and I have now been married almost forty years. We often think back to those earlier days and remember the joy our family has experienced, thanks to making a simple compromise. Of course, we had a little help!

— Carol Emmons Hartsoe —

My Prayer

Dear Heavenly Father, thank you for the many blessings you send our way. We are grateful, Lord, for strength and peace… and for the joy we find if only we will come to you.
Amen.

22

Attitude Adjuster

"Honor your father and mother"—which is the first commandment with a promise—"so that it may go well with you and that you may enjoy long life on the earth."
~Ephesians 6:2-3 (NKJV)

"Would you like to come here and live?" I asked over the phone.

"Yes," she sobbed.

I couldn't believe the words coming out of my mouth as I invited my mother-in-law to live with us. Lillian had never considered me good enough to marry her son. We were now retired and lived five hundred miles away from her home. She had visited, on occasion, with other family members. Now due to her age and ailing health, she needed help. I could not resist her pleading. My husband and I had discussed the possibility of her coming, but he had left the decision up to me.

When I was little, my mom had brought her mother-in-law to live with us. The son she lived with had gone into the Army. As a child, I enjoyed having Grandma there, but knew it was not always easy on my mother.

We moved Lillian into our home. She was pleased with her bedroom and the way I had furnished it.

"Help me keep my focus on you, Lord," I prayed, as the changes started taking place in our home. I knew this would not be easy, as Lillian had never really accepted me, but I understood her feelings for her son. It was not about me, but about her not wanting to share her only child with anyone. I learned to go into my bedroom almost every day and pray, "Lord, please change my attitude so I can be the kind of woman I should be. Help me show love."

At times, it was tense between the two of us. I wanted to honor her even though I was upset. My husband poured out his love for me as I struggled. God let me know that He had faith in me to go on this journey.

The grandchildren enjoyed having a grandma near them. She liked playing games. It was a happy time for her, and I saw the person she wanted to be through the grandchildren. I honored her as the mother of my husband.

At night, my husband and I shared the events of the day. This had become a vital part of our marriage through the fifty years. Many times we would end up laughing at situations that seemed ugly at first. I realized, as I was tested almost daily, that God had strengthened me.

As the years passed, Lillian eventually told me she loved me. I grew to be glad she had come to live with us. I learned how to share my husband with his mother and not make her feel excluded. At one time, we may have been two women competing for the love of one man, but all along there was enough love for all. God is an attitude adjuster; all we have to do is ask Him.

—Beverly LaHote Schwind—

My Prayer

*Dear Lord, thank you for loving me so much that
you take a negative thought and turn it into a
positive word. I pray that you will continue to
nurture all the relationships in my life.
Help me each day to find humor in
situations that seem frustrating and
always remain in your loving service.
Amen.*

23

The Perfect Job

*Pride goes before destruction, a
haughty spirit before a fall.*
~Proverbs 16:18

I was less than a year into my dream job of being a preschool director, but the dream was rapidly becoming a nightmare. My world was crashing, and I was the only one who knew why. It wasn't the job. It was my unrealistic expectation of what I could accomplish, and it was taking a toll on my family—especially the relationship with my husband.

Whenever a staff member did something wrong or a parent disenrolled a child, I blamed myself and took it personally. With a fifty- to sixty-hour workweek, there was little time for family. I felt like a failure at work as well as at home.

I had believed I could do it all. The words "I can't" weren't part of my vocabulary. Besides, how could I confess feeling inadequate to my wonderful husband, who had supported me at every turn? He was so proud of the awards and bonuses I earned, even though I didn't feel I deserved them. I was already letting myself down, and I simply couldn't let him down, too.

With my focus on perfection at the preschool, my husband became both mother and father to our young sons. As he gradually became weary of doing it all, we began to snap at each other. We were growing apart, and I didn't know how to stop it.

As we retired to bed one night, Steve surprised me with a question that made my heart ache. He choked out the words, "Is there someone else?" How could he even think that? I loved him so much, but now I realized that my disappointment in myself had hurt him and our children. Sobbing, I buried my face in his shoulder and admitted my perceived failures. With obvious relief, he responded as I only dared to hope—with love, support, and acceptance.

With Steve's encouragement, I met with our pastor, and his counsel helped me to again put my family first. I vowed never to forget that whatever happens, Steve and I are in it together.

Once my frailties and failures were unburdened, I didn't feel a need to leave my dream job. I remained a preschool director another seven years and was later promoted to the corporate office of the company.

I learned a valuable lesson in my quest to be perfect: "Pride goes before destruction, a haughty spirit before a fall" (Proverbs 16:18). I was blessed that my husband and my faith were both there to catch me.

— Vicki L. Julian —

My Prayer

Father in heaven, please keep me ever mindful that striving for perfection is not the same as expecting to be perfect. Help me to never let pride interfere with the focus on my family.
Amen.

24

Hug 'Em and Pray

Let us then approach the throne of grace with confidence, so that we may receive mercy and find grace to help us in our time of need.
~Hebrews 4:16

"Ma'am, your son is in danger of being expelled." I listen as the Dean of Students expounds on my stepson's seventh-grade hallway misadventures, which bring me to the school at least once a week.

My stepson slouches in his chair, and my heart squeezes at the blank look in his eyes. Where is he? Surely he knows that to be accused of stealing is no small matter. Do I believe everything the Dean tells me, which comes from various sources, or trust everything my son says?

My mom would say there are always three sides to every story: this side, that side, and the truth. Only God knows all three sides. I wish God would share.

As difficult as our beginning together was, I love Taylor. I do not understand him. Ever. We have been in this no-man's-land of step-relationships since he was nearly three years old. Now thirteen, he calls me Mom, having gotten his own mom's blessing before taking that step. We both work hard to maintain a strong, healthy relationship for his sake, and she is a supportive person in our lives. Like a true mom, she seems to know what to do and say at all times.

Oh, that I could be a real mom.

Taylor does not remember a time when I was not part of his life, but sometimes I wonder if he wishes differently. He would never say so. He is often kind, generous, and loving, but there are times when he withdraws and becomes sullen. His bright countenance turns dark, a stranger I don't recognize. Is it the age, or is something more sinister happening?

He is a stranger now. What is he thinking? What would his mom say? I should call her for advice.

Or should I? Isn't this something his dad and I should fix with him? Just where do we draw the line between parents and stepparents? Moms and stepmoms? Of course, I'll call her about the situation, but maybe I should also back away and stop trying to be a mother.

But then I remember who to ask for advice. God is the ultimate parent, a loving presence in spite of our constant backsliding. He can help me reach Taylor and fight the darkness in his eyes.

"Lord, what do I say? What would you say to him?"

My thoughts go back briefly to a small piece of advice our pastor gave us in premarital counseling ten years ago. "When in doubt," he said, "hug 'em and pray."

Taylor sits quietly on the ride home, and I know I must try to offer the comfort God wants to give him. Reaching over, I squeeze his hand. "I love you."

His tough exterior crumbles. Covering his face with one large hand, his voice cracks. "I love you, too."

This time, I know it will be okay. Whatever we muddle through, we'll do it together, with God. Maybe that's what being a real mom is all about.

— Shelley Ring —

My Prayer

Dear Lord, please help my child and me to work out our differences, to communicate better, and to grow in love for one another. May we always see each other as perfect creations of you.
Thank you for being the example we can always look to for help.
Amen.

25

Fighting Words

Don't have anything to do with foolish and stupid arguments, because you know they produce quarrels.
~2 Timothy 2:23

There they were again. My husband's dirty clothes were on the floor, right next to the hamper! Would it have killed him to lift the lid and put the clothes inside? I fumed at this lack of regard for our home's appearance—and for my feelings. I'd asked him nicely in the past to pick up his clothes. I'd teased him that he would make a lousy basketball player. I'd even gotten angry and come just short of calling him a "slob."

But for my husband and me, such name-calling usually just opens up a can of worms. If I criticize his clothes on the floor, he points out all the papers scattered on my desk. So, I remind him that his workbench is a mess, and he says I never clean the crumbs from the counter after preparing sandwiches. Seemingly little issues can blow up into a major ordeal. Therefore, that day I closed my mouth and opened the hamper myself.

I know that my husband and I are not unique when it comes to fighting. Oddly enough, I sometimes wonder if even Mary and Joseph ever fought with each other! I picture them on the long and tiring trip to Bethlehem while Mary was pregnant with Jesus.

After an arduous day of traveling, seemingly in circles, Mary might have said to Joseph, "Why don't you ask that man over there on the camel if we're on the right path to Bethlehem?"

Being a typical man and not wanting to ask for directions, Joseph may have mumbled, "I know where I'm going. You're just crabby because your hormones are raging."

To which Mary would have snapped back, "Well, you'd be grumpy, too, if you were nine months pregnant and riding a donkey all day!"

I guess if Mary and Joseph's marriage could survive the trials they faced in their lives (and certainly their problems were far worse than mine), then perhaps my husband and I have a chance as well. When my feelings escalate to the point of wondering why I ever got married, I know it's time to ask God for help. Sometimes He shows me how to resolve the issue. But other times, there is no easy answer to our disagreement. I realize then that God wants me to swallow my pride, forgive my husband and move on. It's not easy to take that first step toward reconciliation, but it's possible with God's help.

— Susan M. Heim —

My Prayer

Dear Lord, please help my partner and I work out our differences, communicate better, and grow in love and respect for each other as we solve our problems. May we see each other as perfectly created by you—flaws and all.
Amen.

26

My Black-Eyed Susan

*Dear children, let us not love with words
or tongue but with actions and in truth.*
~1 John 3:18

"**W**ill I ever have a positive relationship with my daughter?" I questioned once again.

"Wait until she's twenty-one," a friend advised. "Everything will change then."

Twenty-one? I wanted to enjoy my daughter now. But as Susan struggled with being a teen, a close relationship seemed impossible. We could not agree on anything, and with Susan fighting relentlessly for her independence, we were arguing about everything. Like the flower, my Black-Eyed Susan had always brightened our home. But in her teen years, Susan's dark eyes flashed daggers that could pierce the soul. What happened to my darling little girl? "Oh, Lord," I pleaded, "I want her back! I don't even think she likes me, and I'm not sure I like her either."

"Loving and liking are not the same, Karen," God would whisper in my heart.

I knew I needed to act loving, regardless of how she responded. I wanted to see her through God's eyes. Each time I faced another confrontation with Susan, I would consciously choose to love. It was easier said than done, but each time I asked God for His love to replace my inadequacy, He gave it. Still, clashes were frequent, making my husband and I realize there needed to be space between us. More than once, either by her choice or ours, Susan found herself living with someone else until she wanted to return home.

A few years passed, and Susan became a senior in high school. Our move to Michigan from Florida at that time wasn't easy for her, but somehow Susan sensed that my despondency over the move was stronger than hers, and I began to feel her empathy. Cracks were showing in my veneer of self-sufficiency, revealing a part of me Susan had not seen before. The love I'd chosen to express toward Susan began to once again be returned. A friendship emerged, and we actually found ourselves looking forward to spending time together.

Adjusting to her new surroundings, Susan began to make new friends—and one in particular became that special someone with whom she would choose to spend the rest of her life.

One afternoon, as plans were being made for the wedding, I was overwhelmed by the thought of her leaving. Susan and I had just begun to enjoy each other's company, making up for lost time. I wasn't ready to give her up to someone else.

As Susan continued to talk about her wedding plans, I attempted to put my thoughts aside and concentrate on what she was saying. I tuned back in just in time to hear, "Mom, I want you to be my Matron of Honor. You're the best friend I have."

This time, my Black-Eyed Susan's eyes radiated pure love.

— Karen R. Kilby —

My Prayer

Father, as we struggle in our relationships with our children, help us to see them through your eyes. Your love overcomes any obstacles and barriers that may exist between us. Thank you for giving us the ability to show your love by our actions.
Amen.

27

What a Difference a Day Makes

And let us consider how we may spur one another on toward love and good deeds, not giving up meeting together, as some are in the habit of doing, but encouraging one another...

~Hebrews 10:24-25

The text to my husband read, "Tonight, basketball at 5:30; soccer at 6:30. Which practice are you taking? Dinner will be on the counter." Quick messages here and there represented the majority of our conversations. Life was busy, we were going in different directions, and the family dinner hour was a thing of the past. No longer did we sit around the family table discussing the day's events.

We understood there would be some overlap between interests and sports as our children grew older. But the crazy life we were now leading was solely our fault. We currently had three children on seven sports teams—all at once. Practice was held every night of the week except Tuesdays; games were on both Saturdays and Sundays. The insane schedule was slowly taking a toll on our marriage and family life.

My husband and I grew more distant as the sports season progressed. We fell into the trap of making our children and their lives the priority. We wanted them to be well rounded and healthy, so besides working hard in school, we encouraged their participation in sports. Yet, as their lives were filled with constant activity, our passion for each other diminished to an all-time low. We made halfhearted attempts to talk each day, but most of our conversations centered on the kids. Date nights were long gone. We had almost-perfect attendance on the soccer field, but not in church.

One night after an evening of running around, my husband and I had a heated argument over nothing in particular. That night, I lay awake thinking about our marriage. It was in a state of disarray, and neither one of us was trying to fix it. In the darkened room, I asked God to help us bridge the gap in our marriage. With all we had done to unravel our vows, could He find a way to bring us closer again?

God's answer came the next morning as I was doing the breakfast dishes. We needed to get away together, even for a short time. We didn't have any family close by, so I did the next best thing I could think of: I called a neighbor. She agreed to take the kids for one day. I reserved a room at a beach hotel for the following weekend. I called my husband, instead of texting him, to tell him about my plan. He was thrilled!

The hotel was two hours from our house, so we talked and talked during the entire car ride. We spent more time talking at the beach and throughout dinner. I had forgotten how much I loved my husband's sense of humor and how good it felt to walk hand in hand on the beach. Sharing a cup of coffee on our patio as the sun rose was one of the most romantic things we had done in years. We returned a mere twenty-four hours after we had left, but what a difference that one day had made in our marriage.

— Karen Talcott —

My Prayer

Dear Lord, I ask forgiveness today for filling every nook and cranny of my waking hours with meaningless activities. Help me to simplify my life and remember to spend quiet time with you each day. For it is when we are gentle in spirit that we hear your voice more clearly.
Amen.

28

Please Pass the Spaghetti

So I commend the enjoyment of life, because there is nothing better for a person under the sun than to eat and drink and be glad.
~Ecclesiastes 8:15

"What are you having for dinner tonight?" I asked our daughter, Amber, over the phone. My question was answered with a drawn-out sigh.

"Oh, I think it's a spaghetti night." We both laughed at her response.

When our two daughters were in their teens, we'd faced some challenging times with health issues, career changes, and my husband traveling quite a bit.

One evening as I chatted with my own mother long-distance, I'd suddenly grown serious.

"Mom, what's the secret to putting a little joy into family life? You know how hard it is juggling careers and raising teenagers. Sometimes, it gets a little intense around here."

Mom's words were as surprising as a visit from an unexpected guest.

"Whisper a prayer… then toss some spaghetti at each other once in a while… cooked, that is… Keep things light. Make each other laugh."

That evening, I served pasta for dinner, sharing Mom's advice with my husband and the girls. Mom's idea sounded crazy, even to my own ears. We filled our plates with food, and started sharing our concerns over homework assignments and scheduled appointments for the week ahead. My phone conversation with Mom seemed all but forgotten.

Or so I thought…

As the conversation grew more and more intense, I spotted Amber bowing her head, then reaching for the bowl of spaghetti resting in the center of the table.

"That's odd. Her plate is already full," I pondered silently.

Suddenly, she sunk her fingers into the soft pasta. Lifting several long strands from the bowl, she tossed them high into the air before releasing a loud "Wheeeeee!"

Her actions were met with stunned silence. As we gazed up at the strands of spaghetti dangling from the ceiling, sudden laughter emerged like a volcanic eruption. Throughout the rest of the meal and well into the night, our family experienced one of the happiest, laidback times we'd had in years.

Our daughters, Autumn and Amber, are both married now with families of their own. Thankfully, we're blessed with more days filled with happiness than sadness. But on those days when life becomes a little too intense, we know what to do…

Whisper a little prayer and pass the spaghetti.

— Mary Z. Whitney —

My Prayer

Father God, when our lives are out of balance, we look to you to put everything back into perspective. Your awesome power calms our emotions and restores our sense of well-being. How wonderful it is that even in the midst of chaos, you are a God who appreciates a good laugh.

Amen.

29

Vanity and a Toilet Toupee!

And why do you worry about clothes? See how the lilies of the field grow. They do not labor or spin.
~Matthew 6:28

My mother had cancer and underwent chemotherapy, which caused her to lose all of her hair. Since my mother always hated her hair (too frizzy, too thin, and too red), we told her God was giving her a second chance, and that when it grew back in, it would be thick and straight and beautiful.

In the meantime, Mom went in search of the perfect wig. If there was a wig store within a 100-mile radius, we were there! After more than four weeks of constant shopping, she settled on a $500 wig. It was made of human hair, and had a cap like netting to help keep Mom's head cool. It was straight, thick, and a beautiful shade of auburn.

One morning, Mom used her walker to get into the bathroom. She prepared to put on her new wig by placing a stocking cap over her very bald and smooth head. She then put on the wig and adjusted it. She became frustrated because she felt that the hairs were not lying straight, and she asked if I would "fix it." I looked at the wig—a pageboy cut with bangs—and not a hair seemed out of place, which I told her.

"Can't you see that the side and back just don't seem to lay right? Here, you take the pick and fix it," Mom said.

Rather than argue, I thought it easier to take the pick and go through the motions of combing her wig straight. Unfortunately, the pick caught the wig's netting just right, and the wig flew off my mother's smooth head, leaving the stocking cap in place. The two of us watched in horror as it flew through the air, seemingly in slow motion, heading right for the toilet bowl! With both hands on her walker, my mother kept exclaiming, "Oh, my! Oh, my!"

All the while, I kept thinking, "Where are we going to get the money to replace this $500 rat... I mean, wig?!"

Mom was between me and the bowl, and there was nothing we could do but watch as the wig hit the toilet seat, teetered for a moment, and then fell... onto the tile floor! We both looked into the mirror at each other and burst out laughing. We realized that physical beauty is fleeting, but seeing the humor in life is a gift from God.

—Loretta D. Schoen —

My Prayer

Abba Father, help us to remember that our heart and soul need care, for they are what make us beautiful! When our outer appearance becomes a source of strife, may we recall that we are all beautiful in your sight. Physical beauty may be temporary, but the beauty within us will never die.
Amen.

30

God Has a
Sense of Humor

...he who appoints the sun to shine by day,
who decrees the moon and stars to shine by night,
who stirs up the sea so that its waves roar—
the LORD Almighty is his name.
~Jeremiah 31:35

God does have a sense of humor. Plain and simple, He enjoys a good laugh. Look around you and see the humor in our lives. Then think back to that one time when all hope was lost, when you were down to your last dollar, or you saw no way out. Then suddenly, unexpectedly, things were resolved. The resolution may not have been the direct answer to your question, but it was a way to close one door and open a new one.

There was a time when I was in college that I thought I would fail physics. Maybe "fail" is too strong a word, but I did not want to make anything less than an A in college. I was driven to achieve a certain GPA, but this physics class was on the verge of giving me not only a C, but potentially a D. I was devastated to say the least.

In my despair, I went to Sunset Cliffs one evening to complain to God. I took up my position along the cliffs about twenty feet up from the beach and stood there watching the sun set over a rather peaceful ocean. And then I began to complain bitterly about my lack of understanding and why God was not allowing me to achieve an A in physics.

It was then that God answered me... Distinctly, I heard His words to me, "It is going to be all right. Stop complaining." Then suddenly, out of a calm sea, a wave splashed up on the side of the cliff and drenched me! I looked around, and I was the only one there! And I laughed and laughed... God has a sense of humor after all. You know, I never did get that A, but I did pass the class without issue and never looked back.

To all of you who strain to believe, God is there. He listens. And when we are complaining about nothing, He might even show you His sense of humor!

—Charles Lee Owens—

My Prayer

Father, I place my worries and fears into your mighty hands today. Lead me on the right path and let me plainly see what to do. I thank you for the joy you put into each day.
Amen.

31

Picture Perfect

"Therefore I tell you, do not worry about your life, what you will eat or drink; or about your body, what you will wear. Is not life more important than food, and the body more important than clothes?"
~Matthew 6:25

"Someday, this will be funny." That was my thought as I fumed, looking at my daughter, Mindy, in her ratty pink sweatshirt. I told myself not to make a big deal out of it, to quit being so superficial and prideful. But I was still ticked.

We were getting ready for a family photo for our church directory, and I was quite proud of my little ensemble. I had carefully selected color-coordinated clothes for the five of us—my husband, myself, our two sons, and the aforementioned nonconformist. In varying combinations of red, black, and white, my little clan would be fit for the cover of any parenting magazine. I could just envision this perfect photo on our next Christmas card and the admiration from those who saw how together we were. Totally with it!

I never guessed that Mindy, who detested the itchy black sweater with the tiny red pin dots, had left it behind and was wearing instead her beloved pink sweatshirt hidden from my view under a winter coat. By the time this was revealed at the church, there was no time to return home before our scheduled appointment. I knew that if put to a vote, no one would side with me on the idea of rescheduling. I was the only one who cared.

I'm not sure what bugged me more—the open defiance on Mindy's part or the chagrin that I felt as we posed before the camera, squeezing out forced grins. No matter how much I told myself to chill out and not be one of "those" kind of mothers, my disappointment showed, and the kids all knew it. When the photos came back, I rolled my eyes. As an exercise in humility, I went ahead and had it made into Christmas cards and sent them out. Someday, I hoped, Mindy would see what I saw in the picture, and we would laugh.

That day has come. She's now in her twenties, and the photo recently showed up in an anniversary collection.

"That sweatshirt really did look dumb, didn't it?" she chuckled.

Truth is, it looks no dumber than my huge eyeglasses and hairstyle. The photo would be funny now regardless of whether the whole family had complied. But it would never have had the memorable story behind it of a strong-willed little girl and a controlling, proud woman who have since grown to be friends. A subsequent family portrait, taken some seven years later, sits on a table in our living room. It shows the same five people all in their favorite sweatshirts—strangely enough, color-coordinated—and looking thoroughly comfortable and happy just to be together. I guess Mom learned a thing or two about what she can and cannot control.

When things don't go as I planned, I try to remember that family photo. If it's going to be funny someday, why not today?

— Terrie Todd —

My Prayer

Lord, help me remember what will really matter in the long run and to not sweat the small stuff. Help me create precious moments for my family today that will far exceed any picture-perfect vision I might have for us.
Amen.

32

Magical Mirth

A cheerful heart is good medicine...
~Proverbs 17:22

I t was a rainy evening in December. School was out for the holidays, and after a long day of shopping, my six-year-old daughter was wound tighter than a top.

Seeking solitude from her silliness, I put on a pot of coffee and retired to the den. All was quiet as I collapsed on the sofa in front of a smoldering fire.

Just as drowsiness set in, I was startled by a burst of laughter coming from Leslie's room. Quite frankly, I was annoyed at being disturbed so soon, and I prayed she didn't venture anywhere near me.

But, alas, within minutes, the laughter floated up the hall toward my haven of rest.

Cracking open one eye, I saw Leslie in the doorway, looking like a missile at countdown. An old walking cane was in her left hand, a poncho swallowed her tiny body, and a pair of sunglasses rested low on the bridge of her nose.

With her eyes glued to mine, she hobbled to the fireplace, plopped down on the hearth, and stared. I had no clue who she was pretending to be, and I had no desire to find out.

After several minutes of silent staring, I felt an uncontrollable case of the sillies come over me as well. Sitting up on the couch, I held out my hand for the cane, which she relinquished without a blink.

Trying not to smile, I pointed it in her direction and announced my intention of casting a spell. True, I didn't believe in spells, but it was a nice thought for one exhausted mother. "This spell," I said, in a very serious tone, "will make you fall on the floor and take a nap."

Leslie didn't crack a smile as I recited a hocus-pocus phrase, moving the cane in small circles, mere inches from her nose. At the end of my magical gibberish, I hollered, "FALL!" hoping she would do exactly that.

Just as the word left my lips, a log in the fireplace crashed to the bottom of the grate with a mammoth boom. After shrieking in terror, my silly girl and I fell to the floor and laughed until we cried.

A nap didn't follow as I had initially hoped, but it no longer mattered. The laughter had produced a little magic of its own. No more stress. No more frayed nerves. No hocus-pocus required.

—Gayle Allen Cox—

My Prayer

Dear Father, at times, the child you gave me to raise eradicates my good cheer. But in one magical moment, she brings it all back again, and I feel restored. Thank you for those moments in our lives that we can cherish forever.
Amen.

33

A Merry Heart

*He will yet fill your mouth with laughter
and your lips with shouts of joy.*
~Job 8:21

Mother's Day was quickly approaching. Like many people, we had been adversely affected by the economy. Living paycheck to paycheck, our savings account evaporated into thin air. There was no extra money for anything. It has always been a tradition for Easter that I get a new dress to parade around in like a vain peacock. Well, when I became a mother for the first time, my husband thought it only appropriate to get me a new dress on Mother's Day, as well. But I knew that no new dress would be coming for me this year. We had been creative in making eggs into fifteen different recipes, and hot dogs were our new T-bone steak. Life had thrown us some lemons and, frankly, we weren't lemonade drinkers.

I tried not to get discouraged. "Our rainbow will come soon," I kept assuring myself, but it seemed that lightning struck everywhere I stood. I was getting tired of being frazzled and squeezing every bit out of those lemons.

Mother's Day was my day—a whole day dedicated to me—and I was dreading it. When I woke up that day, the only thought I could muster was, "What kind of eggs will I make today?" But there was a card on the table. On the outside of the envelope it stated, "Enclosed is a few dollars for a new dress. Enjoy." My heart started pitter-pattering twice as quickly as normal, and I thought, "Craig must have been setting money aside."

I opened the card and pulled out a check for one thousand dollars! In the memo, it stated that the money was for a new dress and shoes. I've never spent more than fifty dollars on a dress, so I knew something was up. I looked on the back of the envelope, and it stated, "P.S. Please don't cash for three more years."

I burst into laughter. But as I read the card, my husband's words were so warm and encouraging that I began to cry. We went to church that day, and although I was in old clothes, I radiated with joy and gratitude because I was clothed in love and laughter. I found that I was rich, even living on eggs. After that day, I began squeezing those lemons cheerfully, and soon we all enjoyed the taste of lemonade. I found this plaque at a store and put it in our home: "The happiest people don't necessarily have the best of everything; they just make the best of everything they have."

— Jennifer Smith —

My Prayer

Father, thank you for the medicinal power in laughter. Thank you that, even in difficult times, we can be optimistic, have joy, and laugh. May we find ourselves making the best out of whatever situation you place us in.
Amen.

34

Love in a JCPenney Catalog

And now these three remain: faith, hope and love.
But the greatest of these is love.
~1 Corinthians 13:13

I scanned the pages of the JCPenney catalog as our children slept. My husband was working the night shift, and this was the only way I could finish my Christmas shopping. I checked off items on each child's wish list. I tried not to think about how much I was about to add to my charge card. I flipped through the pages of children's clothing and drifted to the toy section to pick out a few items.

Ron and I had been married five years. Our blended family included his two girls, my four boys, and our toddler son. We both worked hard to provide a home for our children, but the past year had been clouded with arguments and resentment. Everyone in the family was adjusting to the challenges that so many blended families experience, including alimony, child support, and shared weekends. Each one of these challenges seemed to lead to a new argument, and I was having a difficult time pretending to be joyous about the Christmas season.

I let out a sigh and thought back to a day, five years earlier, when

Ron and I had gone to marriage counseling.

"The average blended family takes five to seven years to gel," said the counselor.

"Hmmm," I mumbled.

"That is, if your marriage lasts that long. And only if you both have the support of your ex-spouses."

I glanced over at Ron. Oh, boy. Five years? Who has that kind of patience?

Ron took my hand. "What we need is the six-month plan, Doc," he said. "That's why we're here. We have seven children depending on us. This needs to work now, not five years from now."

She stared back at us. "I see. Well, good luck to both of you."

Five years had passed since that counseling session, and I had lost my enthusiasm for this marriage. Darn, she was right, I thought.

I thought about a recent argument with my stepdaughter that had escalated to an all-out screaming match. I had tried to be the perfect mother, stepmother, and wife, but I had been falling short of that goal for many months.

I flipped to the back of the catalog. On page 758, my eyes were immediately drawn to a wall tapestry with the same dusty rose and green colors of my bedroom. I reached over to the nightstand and grabbed my reading glasses. I leaned in closer to the page. My heart raced as I read the words from 1 Corinthians 13 in the center of the tapestry:

"Love is patient and kind, love is not jealous or boastful; it is not arrogant or rude."

I remember these words, I thought.

"Love does not insist on its own way; it is not irritable or resentful."

I took a deep breath and read further.

"It does not rejoice at wrong, but rejoices in the right. Love bears all things, believes all things, hopes all things, endures all things."

My chin dropped to my chest, and tears ran down my cheek. Finally, I started giggling.

"Sending your love through a JCPenney catalog? Well, God, that's different!" I laughed as I glanced up.

I ordered clothes and toys for the children for Christmas—and the tapestry for our room.

Ten years have passed since that evening, and the tapestry still hangs on a wall in our bedroom. It is a constant reminder of God's unfailing love and our unconditional love for one another. We have had our challenges, but we continue to grow stronger in our love and respect for each other. We count our blessings, and we continue to believe, hope, and endure all things together. We are a family.

— Meagan Greene Friberg —

My Prayer

Lord, thank you for your unconditional love and patience. It is through your love that I find strength. Lord, I ask for continued blessings for my family, in Jesus's name.
Amen.

35

A Fair Sense of Humor

Our mouths were filled with laughter, our tongues
with songs of joy. Then it was said among the nations,
"The LORD has done great things for them."
~Psalm 126:2

After thirteen years of trying to have a baby the old-fashioned way, and being unsuccessful at achieving our goal, my husband Dan and I decided to pursue adoption.

At one point in the process, we had to meet with the adoption agency's social worker individually. Dan went first, and I waited in the lobby. Our social worker was new to the adoption agency and was still getting accustomed to their forms and way of doing things. As a result, while she was friendly to us, she was also very serious and "all business," concentrating very hard on the task at hand.

Dan sat down at the table across from our social worker, and she proceeded to ask him questions. "How would you describe your complexion?" Never in a million years had Dan expected to be asked that question, and he was quite unprepared to answer. Being caught completely off-guard, he thought for a moment, and then, with the sense of humor my husband was blessed with, replied seriously, "I don't know. Ruggedly handsome?" He flashed a charming smile in her direction.

He thought he would get a laugh or at least a smile in return, but our social worker's face scrunched up, her eyebrows knit together, and a frown formed on her mouth. She looked over the top of her laptop screen. Her eyes studied Dan for a moment, and then she looked back down at her keyboard and said in monotone, "I think we'll go with 'fair.'"

Dan told me later he knew in that moment that: 1) Once I heard about what had happened, he would be no less than dead meat, and 2) our social worker was never going to give us a baby.

Of course, while he was dead meat with me for a time, our social worker did give us a baby, and now we have a wonderful laugh with her about that moment! Turns out, my charming husband made quite the impression on our social worker, and she said she will never forget her "ruggedly handsome" client.

Sometimes, in marriage, you just have to make light of things and laugh your way through them, especially when you are in unfamiliar territory or feel completely out of your element. If we have truly placed our marriage in God's hands, He will write our story so that the ending is always a part of His perfect will. And so that, upon the telling, our story glorifies Him.

—Amy L. Stout —

My Prayer

Dear God, thank you for giving each of us a unique sense of humor. Help us to value the differences in personality that we have and to realize that, because of you, we are a perfect complement to one another. Use our story to bring honor and glory to you, and help us to laugh along life's journey. Amen.

36

The Doughnut Disaster

For the kingdom of God is not a matter of eating and drinking, but of righteousness, peace and joy in the Holy Spirit because anyone who serves Christ in this way is pleasing to God and approved by men.
~Romans 14:17-18

I promised my children that we were going to make homemade doughnuts one Saturday morning. I dusted off my Betty Crocker cookbook and found a recipe for cake doughnuts. Luckily, I had all the ingredients in our pantry and began the process in anticipation.

Now, anytime you try to cook with three young helpers, there is going to be some chaos involved. Things are going to spill, messes are going to be made, and some fairness issues will have to be worked out. It is during these moments that I realize I have some control issues.

I wanted this to be a wonderful bonding time with my children, as we filled the kitchen with the fragrant smells of cinnamon and sugar. But it soon became more about who had a turn mixing and pouring in the ingredients.

Then when it came time to cook the doughnuts, my children decided they were done and proceeded to watch TV. I cooked up the remaining doughnuts and then presented them with great flourish on a plate. Each child took one bite and then expressed that they didn't taste like Dunkin' Donuts. Their disappointment registered on their faces, and I felt let down from the whole experience.

It was my husband who came in to rescue the situation. He said to me, "Do not focus on the end result, but instead be happy with the time you spent with your children."

It was exactly what I needed to hear. I had made a memory with my children that morning in the kitchen. I had passed down tips in baking that I had learned from my own mother. God was there in that moment as He is there in all the moments, great and small. The experience changed in my mind, and I was able to see the humor and the love that were there all the time.

— Karen Talcottt —

My Prayer

God, how wonderful you are to give us so many pleasures in this lifetime. Help me each day to find humor in situations that seem frustrating and always remain in your loving service.
Amen.

37

That Praying Family

*Therefore, whoever humbles himself
like this child is the greatest
in the kingdom of heaven.*
~Matthew 18:4

I t was the tail end of our little family getaway, just my children and me. We were tired, cranky, and aching for home and our own beds. We stopped in Reno at a circus-themed hotel for our last "hotel night."

Our first stop was the restaurant. When the food arrived, I reached for my napkin and watched all but one of my kids reach for their forks. Glancing over at my five-year-old, I was surprised to see him sitting quietly. (He does NOTHING quietly.)

"We need to pray," he said.

My little one's clear blue eyes told me he was very serious about this. My other children immediately grasped the situation and began to giggle at the thought of praying right here in Reno, Nevada, in the middle of a circus/casino/restaurant.

"My turn," Noah told us. Then he solemnly closed his eyes and began his prayer.

I felt a giggle coming on, too, and had to suppress it. I knew we were most likely the only people who had ever prayed in this place.

But I also struggled to control my mirth because Noah is deaf, his prayer was entirely in sign language, and he is very expressive! My giggles were quickly replaced with tenderness as my heart swelled with pride. Noah blessed the food and gave thanks for it, but he also blessed his mommy, his kitty, the hotel, his fork, trains in general, his grandparents, our car's tires, and pretty much anything and anyone he had ever met.

I felt the people seated around us grow silent as Noah prayed. And as I watched his little hands talking to God, tears filled my eyes. How blessed I am to be the mother of this incredible little spirit! The silence around us was magnificent as everyone in the restaurant watched a child offer a prayer. I wondered how many of them had ever witnessed a prayer in sign language, let alone in this unlikely place. I felt the Lord's presence with us, and a warmth and sense of immense joy settled around me. As the prayer continued, I realized what an example we, as a family, were setting. And I felt ashamed that I hadn't thought of praying as we normally do at each meal.

As the "amens" rounded our table, I stole a peek at the tables around us. An elderly man with Elvis sideburns mouthed "amen" to me, and his smile told me that Noah's prayer had touched more than my own heart. Everyone at the restaurant seemed to sense the same peace, and the meals were eaten with quiet reverence. As the man with sideburns passed our table on the way out, he gave Noah a thumbs-up—the universal sign for "good job." Noah grinned at the man, spaghetti sauce on his cheeks, even though he had no idea of the impact he'd had on the man. I know it will be a while before that man forgets Noah or his prayer.

After dinner, it fully hit me what a difference my little guy's prayer had made in this corner of the world. A circus act was beginning, and the kids and I crowded in to see. As I held Noah up for a better view, a lady crowded in next to us. Glancing at me, she put her arm across my shoulders and said, "Oh! You're that praying family!"

I looked at my golden boy, smiled, and couldn't think of anything better to be. That praying family.

— Susan Farr-Fahncke —

My Prayer

Dear Father, let me show in my everyday life that there is no wrong time or place to pray; you are always listening. Help me to remember that I am an example to those around me. And through my actions, they may come closer to you.
Amen.

38

A Wrinkled Kiss

God is not unjust; he will not forget your work and the love you have shown him as you have helped his people and continue to help them.

~Hebrews 6:10

I was not nervous, but neither did I know what to expect. I was taking my children to a nursing home to serve the residents. It was an opportunity presented through a group of people in my church who regularly reached out in love to the elderly. Though my children, ages seven and five, had not been around older people very often, I was pretty sure they would be comfortable enough to interact positively without being too frightened.

We were asked to help the residents paint a pot for their garden, and then serve cookies and coffee. My kids are always up for a craft project, and anything having to do with paint especially excites them. They gladly plopped down at one of the tables next to the residents and began to paint little animals onto the clay pots, with minimal apprehensive glances at the shaking hands painting beside them.

It was during "snack time"—as my son, Josiah, endearingly referred to it—that I was stunned and filled with pride all at once. After passing out cookies, my children finished their crunchy sweets in no time, and began to follow me as I meandered and mingled among the residents. If you've ever been to a nursing home, you'll be able to relate to the fragrant wet-diaper-mixed-with-antiseptic-soap-and-Bengay smell that permeated our noses, even as we tasted the cookies. For me, a former certified nursing assistant, it was no big deal, but I feared that my kids and their hypersensitive young noses were not going to tolerate the environment much longer.

It was then, while I was predicting how many more minutes they would last before whining to go home, that I observed one of the most beautiful things I've ever seen. No matter how long I live, I'll never forget it.

One particularly fetid woman had taken a fancy to my son, even being so bold as to hold his hand and squeeze his cheeks. (My son is extremely handsome, bearing the cutest freckles splayed across his sweet little face.) She would beckon him over to her if he wandered too far away. The lines were etched so deeply in her face that I guessed she must have been at least ninety-five years old. Her hands held the beauty of age spots and long, twisted fingers that shook when she reached up to touch him. I was just about to retrieve our jackets and tell them it was time for us to leave when this lovely, endearing woman pointed to her face and puckered her lips to ask him for a kiss.

I felt my eyes widening in curiosity at what he would do. While I could not condone any disgust or rudeness from my son, neither could I force him to do anything awkward or embarrassing. And while I stood there pondering my next move, Josiah amazingly and without hesitation reached out, braced his hand on her wheelchair, and puckered his own pink lips to meet hers. Gentle. Sweet. Unafraid. A smile filled her ancient face, and her delight shone just as bright as if she were decades younger. My charming son could not help but smile in response. Needless to say, my proud tears slid down to the upturned corners of my mouth.

We left that day different from when we had arrived. God had revealed His tender love through my son's courage and grace. It is a wrinkled kiss I'll never forget.

— Robyn Langdon —

My Prayer

*Today and every day, Father, let me show others
what unconditional love and compassion look like.
Through my acts, may they know I belong to the
family of God.
Amen.*

39

Why Didn't I Think of That?

"If you believe, you will receive whatever you ask for in prayer."
~Matthew 21:22

When my oldest daughter, Kaylee, was five, my three younger children attended a "Mom's Day Out" program at our church. This allowed Kaylee and me to spend two whole mornings a week together—just the two of us. Yellow buses, lunchboxes, and Kaylee's first pair of school shoes were just around the corner, so I planned our days carefully. I hoped to show Kaylee God's presence in her life before I had to send her off to kindergarten. We filled our time with walks through trees ablaze in fall colors. We took trips to the zoo, where we discovered new facts about God's creation. We even handed out homemade valentines at a nursing home.

Our house was thirty miles from town, on three lush acres, situated atop a hill overlooking the entire county. Kaylee and I spent many of our mornings enjoying that view from the rocking chairs on our wraparound porch. After one morning, we were getting ready to pick up my younger kids from "Mom's Day Out" when I realized my keys were missing. I usually kept my keys in my van in the garage because keeping keys inside the house was way too risky. My younger boys, like the raccoons in our woods, were fascinated with shiny objects. I had previously rescued my keys from a heater vent, a sandbox, and even the dreaded toilet. Since my keys were not in the van, I assumed my boys had discovered them.

Kaylee and I looked everywhere, but my keys were officially lost. Panic-stricken, I called our church and told them I was going to be late picking up the kids. After I got off the phone, possible solutions raced through my mind. My husband was out of town, so he was no help. I didn't have neighbors near enough to give us a ride. Even if I did, I couldn't ask them to drive half an hour each way. I was considering a taxi when Kaylee's voice broke through my thoughts.

"Mama, the only thing left to do is pray."

"Why didn't I think of that?" I thought to myself.

We held hands, and she prayed six simple words: "Dear God, please fix this. Amen."

When she lifted her head, there was a twinkle in her big brown eyes.

"Mom," she said, "what about the old red truck?"

I explained to her that we had the keys to it, but that really didn't matter because it hadn't run in a long time. She insisted that we try it anyway. I figured it wouldn't hurt to test it, even though I was sure it wouldn't start. We headed across the field and climbed in the truck. I turned the key. The truck sputtered, spit, and then—died. Kaylee begged me to try again, only this time she wanted to pray first.

"God," she said, "we really need you to fix this. Amen."

I smiled and turned the key. The truck sputtered, spit, and then—started! I was so surprised that I laughed out loud.

Kaylee squealed, "I knew it! I knew He could fix anything, Mom." Believe it not, that rusty old truck got us all the way to town and back.

I still laugh when I think about that day. Despite all my plans, it was Kaylee, with her childlike faith, who showed me just how near God really is.

—Leah Clancy—

My Prayer

Thank you, Lord, for your continual presence in our lives. Please bless us with child-like faith and remind us that you are ready and willing to "fix" anything we ask you to.
Amen.

40

Like a Child

And he said: I tell you the truth, unless you change and become like little children, you will never enter the kingdom of heaven.
~Matthew 18:3

The start of a new school year always brings a return to routine at my house. It's the same routine practiced all across the country: roust the children out of bed, make sure everyone has eaten, check to see that the five-year-old has her shoes on, see that hair and teeth are brushed, distribute lunches or lunch money, grab the book bags, and race for the door. Little thought is required for routine. As a mom, I just get in the zone and get it all done. The mental clock is usually ticking the whole time.

One recent morning proved an exception. "The trees are dancing!" exclaimed the five-year-old as we pulled out of the driveway. Her conversation about dancing trees and their choreography went on for about two minutes before I finally came out of my "accomplish the routine" mindset and noticed the amount of wind that day.

Oh! The trees *were* dancing! I was so busy with my routine that I failed to notice the world around me. Once I started paying attention to the movement of the leaves and the beauty of the trees "dancing," it changed my whole mindset.

Experiencing life through the eyes of a five-year-old brought beauty and appreciation back to my morning. I often find it easy to lose the sense of wonder for God's creation that I had as a child. The same is true of my relationship with God. The longer I've been in "the routine," the more likely I am to lose some of the wonder, the awe, and the freshness. It took a young child to remind me that I need to stop and enjoy the wonder of my relationship with God and His creation.

— Deborah L. Kaufman —

My Prayer

Dear Father, renew that sense of wonder and child-like faith that I had when our relationship first began. Remind me to stop and watch the trees dancing or the beauty of a sunset in your creation. But, especially, help me to keep the sense of wonder in my relationship with you, my Creator.
Amen.

41

A Conversation with God

But when you pray, go into your room, close the door and pray to your Father, who is unseen. Then your Father, who sees what is done in secret, will reward you.

~Matthew 6:6

When my son Ben was eight years old, I faced a difficult dilemma. Ben couldn't pass the standardized achievement test due to his dyslexia. So, according to state guidelines, he would have to be "retained" in third grade. Ben's self-esteem was already low, and I worried that "flunking" third grade might damage his fragile ego. Still, my only alternative was transferring him to a private school and pulling him away from the only school he'd known.

Every Sunday, I filed into church and dutifully recited memorized prayers, hoping to receive some divine wisdom. But, week after week, the school dilemma remained.

Then, one day, Ben bounced down the stairs and joined me in the kitchen.

"Guess what?" he said. "I know where you can hear God."

I set down the dishes and smiled at him. "Really?" I asked. "Where is that?"

I expected Ben to say he heard God in church or during catechism class where he was learning the Lord's Prayer. Instead, Ben put his hand to his heart.

"You hear him right here, Mommy," he said, looking down at his chest.

Ben's answer took my breath away.

"You're right!" I replied, feeling a warm blush cross my cheeks. "And what did God say to you?"

"Well, I built my Lego fort first," Ben began. "Then I lined up my Lego people..." He gazed off into the distance, remembering the hundreds of intricate blocks he'd assembled and the figurines he'd placed so perfectly. "Then I just decided to ask Him. 'So, God, how do you like my set-up?'"

I smiled, trying to imagine how God might've answered that question. Did He praise Ben's hard work or command him to obey his parents and clean up his messy room? But the answer was much simpler than that.

"God said I needed more red men," Ben explained.

Ben thought about it for a moment, and then he bolted upstairs where he and God spent the afternoon hunting underneath the bed for more red men.

Ben had a way of doing that—of reminding me about things I should've already known. In the weeks that followed, I began having my own conversations with God. Nothing formal or rehearsed. Just conversations. Questions about what to do next. In time, I began to hear answers in my own heart.

The next year, we transferred Ben to a private school for students with learning differences. His reading skills steadily improved, and his self-esteem grew. He began winning reading awards and speech contests and nabbing lead parts in the school plays. Over time, it became clear that transferring schools had been the absolute right decision.

Ben will be starting high school next year, and again I find myself facing a difficult school selection. But this time, I know just what to do. I think I'll have another conversation with God. I bet He can point me to a good high school with a few red men.

—Madeleine M. Kuderick—

My Prayer

Thank you for hearing our prayers, no matter how great or small they may seem. Thank you for caring about our problems and helping us to find solutions that bring us a sense of peace.
Amen.

42

Bouquet of Weeds

"But the one who received the seed that fell on good soil is the man who hears the word and understands it. He produces a crop, yielding a hundred, sixty or thirty times what was sown."
~Matthew 13:23

My son, Doug, loves weeds. He loves weeds as much as clouds love the sky! He taps them. He folds and molds them. I've even found them under his pillow. The one nice thing about it is that he isn't particular; he likes any color, size, shape or form.

"Doug, what are you doing with that weed in the house?" I questioned impatiently one spring day. "I'm cleaning, and I've already thrown away a big handful of weeds that I've found all over. Now take that old thing outside and don't bring another one in the house. Do you understand?"

"All right!" exclaimed Doug, with a look of persistence in his eyes. "But they aren't just old things. Anyway, why did God make 'em?"

As Doug turned his back and marched out into the yard with his treasure, I pondered the question on his six-year-old mind, knowing he wanted and expected an answer from me. Why does God make weeds?

"So," Doug said, reentering the house and placing his hands firmly on his hips, "why did God make 'em?"

I knelt beside Doug and took his hands. "I think God made weeds for little boys to enjoy. I think He knew that you would be one of the special ones who would love and find beauty in weeds."

A big smile spread across Doug's face. I could tell that he burned with that inner glow of feeling special, something we all need to experience, whether we are two or seventy-two.

"You see, Doug, not everyone thinks weeds are beautiful. It takes a special eye to see their beauty."

"Do your eyes like 'em, Mom?"

"Well, my eyes do, but I like them best outside because I don't like to pick them up all over the house. Maybe you can pick them, plant them, and play with them outside. I think I'd like them even more."

"Okay," was Doug's unconcerned reply as he turned and flew back out of the house.

Did our little conversation work miracles? Are you kidding? I still find weeds in the house, but I don't get upset about it anymore. I realize that, somewhere in our childhood, most of us are fashioned into what others think we should be and should like. As adults, we no longer find time to view the world through the eyes of a child, or see the beauty and purpose of weeds. My son sees weeds just as they are. He does not question their beauty but rather their entitlement to be a part of God's plan.

I have just received a lovely gift from my son: a bouquet of weeds. I shall put them in a crystal vase and place them on our dinner table where we will say grace, thanking God for family, food… and weeds.

— Kathie Harrington —

My Prayer

Dear God, what a blessing it is that our children can see the beauty in an ordinary weed. I admire how they look beyond the flowers and find the good in even the simplest of plants. Help me to learn from this childlike wonder and see the world as you do—a perfect creation.
Amen.

43

Resting in Hope

Therefore my heart is glad and my tongue rejoices; my body also will rest secure.
~Psalm 16:9

S ometimes, life is just difficult. As a mother, it is frustrating when our children say mean things to each other and fight over toys. It is difficult when the clothes dryer quits and the dog gets sick. And how many times has a day gone by and you realized you forgot to take a shower? Hope helps.

One day, my ten-year-old son Noah and I were driving down a heavily trafficked street when my car started dying and then completely stopped. After a couple of minutes, it started again, only to die once more a block up the street. I pointed the car toward the repair shop, but we stopped and started several times along the way.

Hope leaked out of me like the transmission fluid leaked out of my car. Frustration crept in. By our third stop and start, I was angry.

In tears, I asked, "Noah, will you pray for me?"

My son prayed, "God, please help Mom not be so frustrated and help us make it to the mechanic's. And help Mom know that this is a tiny little problem compared to the rest of the world."

Truth and perspective. My little man was full of hope. When the hopeful help the hopeless, I think God applauds. Giving hope is a beautiful transaction, born of love and selflessness. It is especially lovely when a child gives hope to a parent.

We made it to the auto shop where my car was pronounced dead. Transmission problems. That's like terminal cancer for cars.

At home, my husband and I talked about our situation. Hope must be consciously invited into a discussion of finances when money is tight. It is so easy to give up and dwell on thoughts like, "Can't we ever get ahead?" and "Why do we always end up dipping into savings?" After a tense discussion, John and I prayed and made some decisions. Hope arrived with a plan in his hand.

That night, I hugged my son tightly and thanked him for his prayer in the car. God used my son's words to whack me in the head. Noah was right. The death of a car is not reason to lose hope and despair. Why? Because we have the hope of Christ. We've made a decision in faith to lean on the supernatural, invisible God who allows joy and doesn't always shield pain.

We hope.

If you are discouraged by this economy or by loneliness or by the endless exhaustion of being a mother, I urge you to look up and lie back. Rest in His hope, and He will carry you through. Even when life is difficult.

— Robbie Iobst —

My Prayer

God, thank you for the knowledge that you are in control and will carry us through. Remind me to rest in that hope and then teach it to my children. And help me to listen when my children are the carriers of your divine message.
Amen.

44

Having It All

...the Spirit helps us in our weakness.
~Romans 8:26

When my daughter, Julie, was a first-grader, I was spinning more plates than a circus juggler. Wife, mom, daughter, granddaughter, corporate travel manager, as well as Sunday school teacher, member of the church choir, and assistant troop leader for the Brownies—you could say I had my hands full. Like many young mothers, I'd eagerly bought into the popular 1980s ideal: "Today's woman can have it all."

It wasn't long before I concluded the principle we embraced was a bunch of baloney. Whoever thought it up clearly never tried to do it all, was a native of the planet Krypton, or had one heck of a lot of help crossing the finish line.

Of course, it was possible that I was busy running around in circles on the day that super powers were passed out to the other moms. One thing was certain: There wasn't enough time in my schedule for everything that was crammed into it. Every trip to the car seemed to begin with "Hurry up, we're late!"

And it was bugging me.

On a particularly chaotic day at work, the phones rang off the hook, and I barely stopped long enough to take a sip of coffee. My lunch hour consisted of wolfing down a peanut butter and jelly sandwich, collecting Julie from school, and bringing her back to the office to do her homework while I dove into the pile on my desk.

When it was time to pack up and leave, I was so exhausted that it was all I could do to turn the key in the ignition and put the car in reverse.

Suddenly, Julie gasped in delight and pointed toward the western skyline.

"Mommy, look!"

The sun had set behind the trees, leaving behind smudges and swirls of violet, lavender, peach, salmon, and gold... sublime, breath-taking, soothing, and energizing. I'd never in my life seen such colors.

"Oh, my!" I exclaimed.

There we sat, mother and daughter, mesmerized by a heavenly canvas.

"God must really love us today," said my little girl.

I was deeply touched by her words.

"Indeed," I murmured, stroking her hair, savoring the rare moment of peace that washed over us both.

Later that evening, it occurred to me that I'd been chasing what I already had: a rich, full life with family, home, friends, a great job, a wonderful church. Who could want more? What I needed was someone to help me make sense of it all and keep me sane. Who better than the Giver of Life, the one true Super Power? After all, He was the one who had blessed me in the first place. Through Him, all things are possible. Through Him come strength and rest.

My grandmother used to say, "It's sometimes hard to see the forest for the trees."

How true. When the trees stepped aside, I got a good look at the forest. And it was beautiful.

— Michelle Close Mills —

My Prayer

Heavenly Father, thank you for giving us more than we could ever hope for. Help us to see beyond the busy-ness of daily life, so we may fully recognize your gifts and be truly thankful.
Amen.

45

A Race Run Well

Do you not know that in a race
all the runners run, but only one gets
the prize? Run in such a way
as to get the prize.
~1 Corinthians 9:24

My son, Nick, loves sports: running, hitting balls, shooting baskets, you name it. But what he loves even more is to have his father and me there on the sidelines watching him. So, naturally, for his kindergarten field day, I was there ready and waiting, camera in hand to watch him run the 200-yard dash.

Though it was a sunny May morning, the night before had brought enough rain that the morning sun didn't have time to dry the ground, so it was slick. Seven kindergarten boys were standing at the ready, bodies wiggling in anticipation for the flag to fall. It did, and they ran. Nick pushed his way to the lead and ran for all he was worth. My camera clicked constantly, trying to capture my son's body as it flew past me toward the finish line.

But then he fell, his feet sliding out from under him and across the wet grass. Every mother knows what it feels like when her child falls, whether literally or figuratively. For Nick, that moment in the grass was defining for him. He looked at me bewildered, not sure what to do. Was he going to give up and walk the rest of the way? Would he cry? Would he even finish? I could see the wheels turning furiously in his head.

I started shouting. "Get up! Keep going!" I must have looked ridiculous, shouting and jumping up and down like a maniac with my camera flying around my neck, but it was enough to encourage my son to get up and finish. He did more than finish. He won, propelled by a determination that I had never seen in him up to that point.

I like to think that, as his mom, it was my screaming and jumping that did it. It probably was. After all, he was only six, and I was still cool. But it reminded me at that moment of God, and how He is there to encourage us when we fall, whether it's through a kind word from a friend, through His Word or some other way. God is a God of encouragement. He wants us to succeed. Sometimes, success is just the act of finishing what we've started and not letting the circumstances around us determine how we will behave.

I was so proud of Nick that day—not for winning, but for getting up and doing what needed to be done—the determination, the work, the payoff. May we be willing to do what God has called us to do as moms—to work, be tenacious, and never give up.

— Kathryn Nielson —

My Prayer

*Lord, I pray that you will give me the encouragement
to finish the tasks that you have given me to do in this
life. Please grant me tenacity and the desire to finish
well so that when I see you face-to-face, I will be
able to hear you say, "Well done."
Amen.*

46

The Rainbow Child

"You are the light of the world."
~Matthew 5:14

"It's bad news," my sister, Christie, told me over the phone. "Erik has epilepsy."

I blinked back tears. "Oh, honey, I'm so sorry."

"He's suffered so much," she continued, "and now this dual diagnosis. I guess we'll just have to take it day by day."

"Yes," I said. "And pray."

"And pray."

Her voice stayed with me long after our call. Steadfast in her care of Erik, her twenty-year-old son, my sister was forever his advocate. He would always be the love of her life.

Autistic and very low-functioning, Erik had retreated into his inner world at eighteen months old and not spoken since. He could now communicate basic needs via sign language, but this achievement was exceedingly hard won. There had been countless doctors, programs, and therapies; Erik was poked, prodded, and tested for many years. Through it all, Christie went to great lengths to preserve her boy's unique and gentle spirit. "I don't want his world to be gray," she once told me. "I want him to see rainbows."

Epilepsy had dealt them a crippling double blow, adding a whole new level of complexity to an already complicated affliction. What would Christie and her husband have to do to further care for their only child? Moreover, how could they communicate what epilepsy even was to a young man who couldn't communicate? Erik's seizures must have terrified him. I wished for a way to help, but living nearly a thousand miles away made that impossible.

And then I recalled how Christie and I had ended our conversation, on that invocation to pray. All at once, it seemed the best thing I could do. I set about it the very next morning. As time passed, my prayers became more specific, focusing expressly on Erik and his needs. I added a rosary when I knew he'd be undergoing something traumatic, like a doctor appointment or an adjustment of medication.

One day, as I finished my prayer, I noticed something. There, on the wall across from me, just beneath my back window, was a tiny yet lovely spectrum... a small rainbow. I had seen it before, but it now held special significance. Though fleeting, it seemed to appear when sunlight filtered in through the window at just the right angle, then passed through a mosaic candle holder displayed there. It suddenly occurred to me that light worked hard to produce that spectrum of color. It bent and twisted and refracted, but without the refraction, light couldn't be prismatic. Light, I concluded, must be very brave. Just like Erik and his parents.

Sometimes, situations are simply bigger than we are, and all we can do is face them courageously. Yet if we can arm ourselves with prayer, our days don't feel quite so gray. And sometimes, amidst all the bending and twisting, all the refraction, we are graced with pure light and the presence of a rainbow child.

— Theresa Sanders —

My Prayer

Illness and disability are never easy, Father, but help us to remember that you are the Supreme Healer, the pure and abundant light that brightens our way. Let us look for you not in the grand sweep of sameness, but in the fine and mysterious detail of the unique. When our days are gray and our spirits low, remind us of rainbows.
Amen.

47

The Comfort of Each Other

Praise be to the God and Father of our Lord Jesus Christ, the Father of compassion and the God of all comfort, who comforts us in all our troubles, so that we can comfort those in any trouble with the comfort we ourselves receive from God.

~2 Corinthians 1:3-4

My phone buzzed with an incoming text: "Laura was in a snowboarding accident. She's in the hospital. Please pray."

I stared in disbelief at the message. In a few bland characters, I learned my dear friend was seriously injured. But a glance out the window showed the predicted snowstorm raging in earnest. Large flakes swirled in circles in my backyard. Now was not the best time for a blizzard. But snow or no snow, I had to go. What are friends for if not to weather the worst of life together?

Within the hour, I threw a packed bag into my truck. After exchanging hugs with my husband and children, I backed out of the garage and began a slow trek into the mountains. The blowing snow moved in horizontal lines in front of me, obscuring the roads and fighting me for control.

Soon, darkness fell, and exhaustion settled in. The weeks before had been some of the most difficult I'd faced. A move from our family home, economic challenges, the death of another dear friend, and struggles with our teenagers had replaced peace with tension. During one difficult night, I'd called Laura, desperate for the reassurance of a friend. I spilled my heartache over the phone while she listened, allowed me to cry, and told me she loved me and would always be there for me.

Now, as I crawled over the mountain toward the hospital on the other side, I realized it was my turn to hold her hand, let her cry, and tell her I'd be there for her, as long as it took.

When I arrived, her smile lit up the room. With multiple broken bones, she could do little more than squeeze my hand and allow the tears to fall. Seeing her pain released my own.

"I'm with you, Laura, as long as it takes. We're going to get through this."

And we did. During part of her recovery, she lived in our home, a time so full of laughter, tears, friendship, and healing that I doubt its equal will ever be found this side of heaven. We talked from our breakfast coffee until long after my family retired to bed. We shared stories from childhood, wrestled with the challenges of adulthood, and laughed until her back couldn't bear it. And when either her physical pain or my heart pain became a mountain too big to climb, we soaked in each other's presence until we made it to the other side. And right there, in the middle of life's storms and my living room, we experienced the comfort of each other.

Challenges will still come, storms seemingly too violent to weather, mountains appearing too steep to scale. Every struggle conquered leaves others waiting in line to take its place. But we don't have to live it alone. Thank God, we don't have to live it alone.

— Michele Cushatt —

My Prayer

Thank you, Father, for the comfort you give us through others. Teach us to follow your ways and become a source of strength for those who are also suffering. Let us celebrate the gift of community that you have given us.
Amen.

48

Never Alone

When my spirit grows faint within me,
it is you who watch over my way.
~Psalm 142:3

Loneliness engulfed me as I waved goodbye to my parents. They had spent the past few days helping my children and I move into our apartment, but now they were heading back to their home, a two-hour drive away. I'd left my husband and the first house I'd ever owned to move into a small two-bedroom apartment with my sons, ages four and one. With my parents' departure, the frightening reality hit that I was solely responsible for these little boys and our survival.

My younger son was napping in his crib, and my other son headed out to the screened-in porch in the back of our second-floor apartment. He was excited to see all the ducks swimming in the small lake behind us, but all I could see was despair. I flung myself onto my bed and sobbed my heart out to God, praying for the courage to face the daunting future ahead of me.

After the tears had subsided somewhat, I heard my son speaking to someone. "My name is Dylan," I heard him say. "What's your name?" A female voice responded, and I realized that she must be walking on the ground below. I couldn't hear her response, but my son told her, "I just moved here with my mom and my brother. Where do you live?"

Their conversation continued for a short while, and then it grew quiet. I called Dylan into my bedroom to ask who he had been talking to. "It's a really nice lady, Mommy. She lives right below us, and she has a girl named Jenny who's the same age as me! She said that we can play together anytime."

In the years to come, we became good friends with Jenny and her single mom, Sherry. We took care of each other's children and cats, played with our kids at the park together, and shared the challenges of single parenting. One day, it hit me that God had not left me alone. He'd sent my friendly little boy out to the balcony to bring us some friends. And he'd given me the strength and courage I needed to provide a good life for my family.

—Susan M. Heim—

My Prayer

Dear Father, you assure us that we are never alone. May I seek comfort in your words when I feel lonely or scared. I know that you will never desert me in my time of need and will give me strength to face any situation that arises.
Amen.

49

Quiet in the Midst of Chaos

"Ask and it will be given to you; seek and you will find;
knock and the door will be opened to you."
~Matthew 7:7

Scott's face was as pale as the sheet that was stretched across his chest. The white mound moved up and down with his breath—I watched to make sure. His eyes were large, light blue frightened circles that were searching mine for comfort. I latched onto his hand and squeezed; it was slippery with sweat and unnaturally cold. Bending down to feel his hands against my face, I reveled in his familiar scent and kissed his lips; they were so cold, it chilled me deep down. Tears fell as he spoke. "I'm sorry."

Fear stole my breath, but I managed to say "I love you" as they wheeled him away.

I stood there with my hand trembling in mid-air, staring past the blurry double doors that swung closed, too stunned to move. It had all happened too quickly to fully register in my brain. Severe chest pain; a lightning-fast drive to the ER; a flurry of gloved hands and wires hooked to every inch of his body; doctors rattling off questions while I fumbled for answers; and alarms I barely heard over the pounding of my own heart. I just remember staring at my husband's face and thinking he looked as lifeless as his mother did when I dressed her frozen body for the funeral. This couldn't be happening.

I wandered into the waiting room, alone, more scared than I knew possible, and sat down heavily, barely breathing. The television hummed with action, and an intercom system called out muffled names as the elevator dinged repeatedly. The smell of stale coffee and the weight of grief turned my stomach sour. I was twenty-nine years old and happily married for eleven years, with four small children at home. How does a woman who's not yet thirty face the possibility of becoming a widow? Dear God, I thought, are you even there?

Pulling out my cell phone, I called my mother and sobbed until I couldn't breathe. When I hung up, I didn't feel any better. In fact, panic and doubt had made me hysterical. Pacing the small room like a caged beast, my heart rammed up against my ribcage, and my breath came out in several short bursts. It was late. I didn't want to disturb my friends, my mom and dad lived hundreds of miles away, and my sister was watching my children, but I desperately needed relief. Where could I turn for peace? In my heart, I knew the answer, but I lacked the courage to try.

Knock and the door will be opened to you. I stumbled out into the hallway, where the bright fluorescent lights assaulted my swollen eyes, and searched for a quiet place. Dropping to my knees, I called out to God, pushing aside my fear and relying on a fleeting flicker of faith. In the wee hours of night, I turned my heart to the Father—and He gave me, as promised, His peace.

My husband survived. I will be forever grateful for that priceless gift, and also for His wordless message: In a life of chaos and uncertainty, we must fall to our knees to find the strength to stand.

— Michelle Crystal —

My Prayer

Lord, what a gift it is that you stay with us in our intense trials and never let us go. Even when I am full of uncertainty, your divine presence comforts my soul and brings me peace.
Amen.

50

Two Hearts

Wait on the LORD; Be of good courage, and He shall strengthen your heart; Wait, I say, on the LORD!
~Psalm 27:14 (NKJV)

It was Valentine's Day. Home from work, I headed toward the bedroom, looking for my husband. The sight of two pink chocolate-filled hearts on the bed stopped me in the doorway. My husband turned to face me with a grin. He had been a casualty of employee cutbacks at his job and out of work for a few weeks. Our cash flow had become severely restricted, so we were budgeting carefully. The two small gifts—one for me and one for our daughter—were an extravagance. I felt a wave of nausea come over me as I realized that my news would soon overshadow the sweetness of this thoughtful gesture.

With a heavy heart, I entered the room. Leaning against the dresser, I stood silently with my coat still on, my purse in hand. My eyes brimmed with tears, and my husband's smile sagged into a frown. His blue eyes clouded.

"I just lost my job," I blurted out as the tears began to flow.

"What happened?" he asked, panic in his voice.

My heart cracked. Dropping my purse, I slid slowly down the front of the dresser. Falling to my knees, I wept uncontrollably.

"Debbie, what happened?" he asked again, my silence panicking him even more.

I lifted my face and looked at him. "They didn't need me anymore. Last one in, first one out," I said through my tears. "I have a severance check in my purse, and my personal belongings are still on the back seat of the car."

Dropping to the bed, he barely missed the pink hearts he had so lovingly placed there. For the next half-hour, I relayed the events of the day. His shoulders drooped under the burden I had just placed there. In the end, I sat on the floor, a red-eyed, tear-stained mess, repeating "I'm so sorry."

My husband had soldiered through each day, searching for another job, reviewing our finances, keeping a brave face to steady the family, but I always knew he was hanging on by a thread. I knew my news would only increase the burden on his heart. Finally, he said, "Well, God has always taken care of us in the past. We just need to trust Him now." He pulled me to my feet, and we held each other. Later, we sat down together and restructured our budget, adjusting for my severance check.

A few months later, we both found jobs, and life returned to normal. I must admit, I still cannot look fondly on that Valentine's Day, but now when my life feels out of control, I remember the two pink candy hearts. They remind me of God's faithfulness to strengthen our two hearts as we supported one another and aspired to "be of good courage" while we waited upon the Lord.

— Debbie Acklin —

My Prayer

Dear Lord, I pray that you will always give us the strength to stand in the face of adversity. Please strengthen our hearts for each other during this time and bless us with your "good courage."
Amen.

51

Finding Peace in the Midst of Pain

No discipline seems pleasant at the time, but painful. Later on, however, it produces a harvest of righteousness and peace for those who have been trained by it.

~Hebrews 12:11

One year ago, I was buzzing through life with much to be thankful for. I was thirty-eight years old, had three beautiful kids, a wonderful husband, great friends, great church and great health—or so I thought. Then I felt a lump in my breast and quickly found out it was breast cancer.

In the next twelve months, I went through a double mastectomy, chemotherapy and radiation, and, of course, the loss of all of my hair! I thought my faith was pretty strong, but this shook me to the core. Fear crept in and tried to take hold, but the wonderful, faithful Christians around me wouldn't allow it.

So I grabbed on to the Lord and prayed for my mustard seed of faith to grow and for peace that surpasses all understanding. Of course, I prayed for healing, but I knew that wasn't always God's plan. Through every test result and doctor's appointment, I prayed for God to keep me sane.

I know now that the only way I got through those twelve months was with the Lord carrying me through. Whenever I walked through the doctor's door, waiting for test results, my knees would be shaking. But I would tell myself, "He will get me through," and He always did. Somehow, through all this insanity, I was able to laugh and smile and thank God for so many things.

There was the time I cried out to the Lord, "I cannot wait five days for these test results!" and they came back two days later. And the time when I wasn't sure whether to postpone one of my surgeries for another family emergency when the doctor's office called not an hour after I prayed for guidance and asked if they could reschedule. God is so amazing!

Somehow, I found peace during this difficult time. It was hard, and cancer is scary, but I faced it because I knew that God was working in my life. I'm now done with all of my treatments and surgeries, and I can look back and know that my faith—once the size of a mustard seed—has grown. I learned that God really does give you what you need. When you go through the dark times believing in this assurance, I promise you He will.

—Jennifer Stango—

My Prayer

Dear Father, I know that you hold me in your loving arms whenever life seems too difficult to bear. Help me to find peace when sorrow and fear have me in their grip. Through you, I know I have the strength to come through whatever pain I will experience.
Amen.

52

The Miracle of Acceptance

Shout for joy, O heavens; rejoice, O earth;
burst into song, O mountains! For the
Lord comforts his people and will have
compassion on his afflicted ones.
~Isaiah 49:13

I was almost seven months pregnant and coping with the realization that my husband had relapsed yet again in his alcoholism. This came after an extended period of sobriety, a time of joy and hope, during which I got pregnant. Unfortunately, as so often happens in addiction, the recovery was too tenuous to hold.

One July evening, I walked to a nearby church for an Al-Anon meeting. For once, I was not angry at my husband. I just felt utterly defeated by the disease. That night, I needed the comfort of the familiar Serenity Prayer: "God grant me the serenity to accept the things I cannot change, the courage to change the things I can, and the wisdom to know the difference." I also yearned for the company of others who understood, as perhaps few others can.

This particular meeting was uneventful, actually quite ordinary. I sat there, I confess, mostly lost in my own thoughts. And then it happened: an awareness, I suppose. A warm light flowed completely into my mind and my heart. And with the light came a quiet voice: "You have no control over his drinking." It was not a thought. I now believed and accepted this truth.

I had hoped and prayed for the miracle of acceptance over many years. It set me free. As I walked home, I marveled at how calm and peaceful I felt. I held love in my heart for my husband, seeing his pain and struggle. I also felt clear about my reality. The time for wishing was over. I was going to be raising my child alone, whether I stayed married or not. My husband, so disabled by drinking, would not be able to fully participate as a parent.

I was no longer afraid by that thought, though. I knew, without any doubt, that God and I would walk on this journey together. He would be there to help me make the difficult decisions that needed to be made. And, when it was over, I would walk away with strength I never knew existed inside me.

— K.P. —

My Prayer

God, during those times when we are at our lowest, you somehow find a way to reach down to us. You whisper the very words we so desperately need to hear. Thank you for your enduring love in all the seasons of our lives.
Amen.

53

Broken Bones and Prayers

When I am afraid, I will trust in you.
~Psalm 56:3

July 17, 2009, began like any other Friday. I went out to the barn to feed the animals, and then came back inside to get our daughter out of bed. My husband and four-year-old son hugged us goodbye as they left. Chris would drop Cody off at Grandma's house on his way to work. Cody always looked forward to Fridays with Grandma. They usually spent the morning playing in her kitchen or garden while I worked from home and cared for one-year-old Kayce.

On this particular morning, the phone rang unexpectedly as I was feeding Kayce her breakfast. It was Chris. In a tense voice, he told me there had been an accident at Grandma's house, and Cody was hurt. I pulled Kayce out of the highchair, and we jumped in the car.

Ten minutes later, I arrived to find Cody lying on the living room floor, crying and screaming. His left leg was grossly swollen, and his ribs had begun to turn black and blue. Beside him lay the grandfather clock that normally stood against the wall. The doors to the chime cabinet were open, and the glass face of the clock was shattered. That old, heavy clock had fallen on top of him.

As gently as possible, Grandma picked him up and placed him in the back of my SUV, climbing in beside Cody to support him. I took off for the nearest emergency room a half-hour away. I had never driven so fast in my life. Cody's cries frightened me.

When we arrived, a male nurse lifted Cody directly onto a gurney from the back of the SUV. The ER doctor barked orders to those around him. A short time later, we were given the news: Cody's left femur was badly fractured. X-rays vividly revealed the bone, now splintered at a forty-five-degree angle. My breath caught in my throat as Grandma broke down in tears.

A short time later, we met the orthopedic surgeon who would set the broken bone. He explained that, because of the severity of the break, Cody would need to be in a body cast for at least six weeks. As we walked alongside the gurney toward pre-op, I tried to hold back the tears. I was terrified that Cody had to be under anesthesia for the procedure. I silently begged the Lord to calm my pounding heart. Cody began to cry when the nurse told us we couldn't continue any farther with him. At that moment, I leaned over him and whispered in his ear the words of Psalm 56:3, "When I am afraid, I will trust in you." I repeated the verse several times to him and promised we would be there when he woke up.

The hour and a half in the waiting room felt like years. I spent the time silently repeating Psalm 56:3 over and over. Though anxious, my heart calmed. Cody came out of the anesthesia very well, and our focus turned to learning how to care for him in the body cast.

The next six weeks were a rollercoaster time of good news and bad, triumphs and setbacks, but through it all we gave our fears to the Lord in prayer. When Cody's cast came off, we faced the challenge of helping him learn to walk again, but we made it through by confidently trusting the Lord every day.

— Jenny R. George —

My Prayer

*Dear Heavenly Father, thank you for your strength
of presence when circumstances beyond our control
shake our emotional foundations. You are an oasis
of courage when we are anxious and afraid.
Help us, Father, to always remember
to put our trust in you.
Amen.*

54

The New Teacher

"For this is what the LORD, the God of Israel, says: 'The jar of flour will not be used up and the jug of oil will not run dry until the day the LORD sends rain on the land.'" She went away and did as Elijah had told her. So there was food every day for Elijah and for the woman and her family.

~1 Kings 17:14-15

"Y ou look like you've had a toothache for the last six weeks," said Nancy. "Are you okay?"

"Oh, sure. I'm just tired," I lied, unwilling to admit to a co-worker that my becoming a teacher was a mistake and that I doubted I would last that first year. Making it to November looked uncertain.

During the job interview, I impressed the principal and the English supervisor with confidence and enthusiasm—even when they explained that the students assigned to me would be difficult, and the program lacked a curriculum and books. The supervisor promised, "Don't worry. I'll mentor you. We'll work together."

On the eve of my first day, my mentor handed me a box of discarded books and said, "You might find something useful here." She paused, and then blurted, "Dorothy, I'm sorry. I've accepted another job. I won't be here to help you." She headed to her office to pack, leaving me stunned, though unshaken.

But Day One shook me. Teachers say the first weeks are easy, with students eager to make a good impression. My students' glazed eyes, sullen faces, and rude responses hinted we would have no honeymoon. Still, I believed my upbeat attitude would carry me. But it held no sway over kids biding their time until they could quit school forever. I shopped for motivational strategies and educated myself on teaching at-risk children. But the struggles only escalated. Within two weeks, a lump in my throat and a tightness in my gut were constant.

One Sunday, I was scheduled to read the Scripture passages at church. When I opened my Bible to rehearse, I found the assigned verses in Chapter 17 of the Book of Kings. The widow of Zarephath, expecting that she and her son would die of starvation, received this promise from the prophet Elijah: "The jar of flour will not be used up and the jug of oil will not run dry…" The knot in my stomach loosened at the words, "So there was food every day for Elijah and for the woman and her family." In those words, I detected a sign that translated into "Don't worry. You'll make it until June."

At school, the kids and the job did not change that much. But I did, as I claimed God's promise and faced each day with strength and confidence. Nancy even noticed that I was smiling again. Several weeks later, the principal stopped to say, "I am impressed. Yesterday, I stood outside your door. I never saw a teacher get as much out of those kids as you did."

"Thank you, sir," I answered. But to the One who is truly in charge, I prayed, "Thank you, God, for the graces to recognize that I only have the power to change myself and to know that with your help I can meet any challenge life sets before me."

— Dorothy K. LaMantia —

My Prayer

Lord, help me be mindful that the little things I do every day when I am teaching others, I do for you. Thank you for allowing me to fulfill my spiritual gift of teaching and to become a better Christian in the process.
Amen.

55

The Great Physician

And the prayer offered in faith will make the sick person well; the Lord will raise them up...
~James 5:15

"The test results show you have ovarian cancer."

When I heard those piercing words spoken by my gynecologist, shock and fear enveloped me. Nothing could have prepared me for the extensive exploratory surgery, the four-hour-long chemotherapy treatments over the next several months, or the resulting weakness, hair loss, and extreme stress. Why did this deadly disease attack my body? The question haunted me nearly every day.

According to the surgeon, my prognosis for surviving Stage III(C) ovarian cancer was only 8-13 percent for the next five years. I felt God had abandoned me. Tentacles of palpable loneliness wrapped around my heart. I didn't know of any women who had been stricken with ovarian cancer and lived through it. There were no examples to follow, no hope to be garnered from other humans. Tears were cried in vain... or so it seemed.

In desperation, I turned to the Bible for solace. As I read more and more Scriptures about the love and compassion Jesus demonstrated to those He met, my broken heart slowly began to mend. The account in the New Testament gospels of the woman with horrendous female problems resonated with me. Her hope in Jesus ignited faith, and healing came by simply touching the hem of His garment. If Christ cared enough to stop in His tracks, turn, and tell this woman her faith had made her well, maybe I could believe for my healing, too.

Word of my illness spread quickly among family and friends, and the ripple effect became huge. Prayers from people all over the country were lifted on my behalf.

As I healed emotionally, my body also began to be restored. When each blood test came back from the lab with excellent results, I felt a flood of relief and increased hope.

Finally, after a tough year, I was pronounced cancer-free. A total miracle.

This occurred fifteen years ago. Like the woman in the gospels, I believe my illness and suffering made me reach out to the Great Physician—the only one who could understand as well as triumph over all obstacles.

Cancer forced me to stop and consider what is really important. I do not take my health or anyone else's for granted. I've learned to cherish my relationships with my Creator, family, and friends. These are far more important than the busyness of this life.

— Ann Holbrook —

My Prayer

Father, I pray for those who have lost hope because of their suffering. I ask that you would ignite the flame of faith and empower them to trust in you. In Jesus's name...
Amen.

56

A Beautiful Mess

*Be completely humble and gentle; be patient,
bearing with one another in love.*
~Ephesians 4:2

"He left me," I whispered into the phone. "He said he didn't love me anymore."

"Oh, sweetheart, I'm so sorry," my stepfather, Doug, said. "Your mom and I are here for you. Whatever you need, you can count on us."

When my mother's husband made that promise, I'm sure he didn't realize how much it would involve. I'm sure he didn't plan on having his stepdaughter and her two young children move in with him. But it happened, and he was wonderful about it.

I should have been grateful, but I was too wrapped up in my own pain to notice the sacrifices others were making. I cried a lot and ate next to nothing. Sadly, I abdicated much of my parenting responsibilities to my mom and Doug.

Shortly after moving in, I began to find little notes on my dresser. But they weren't from my mom; they were from Doug. My favorite one read, "If you ever need a shoulder to cry on, the Lord gave me two of them. They're big and strong, and they're available anytime you need them."

I went downstairs and made good use of that shoulder. When I'd finally stopped crying, Doug said, "What's the hardest part of this for you?"

I shrugged. "My life is a mess."

"You may see a mess, but God sees it as an opportunity for growth. He's molding your heart and drawing you to Him. It may be a mess, but it's a beautiful one."

I was definitely a mess, but there was nothing beautiful about it.

In the silence, Doug added, "God isn't nearly as concerned with where we've come from as He is with where we're going. And you're heading in the right direction, honey."

I muttered a thank-you and went back upstairs.

Two days later, I found a small plaque in my room. It read, "God gave you 86,400 seconds today. Have you used one of them to say thank you?"

I wanted to ignore the little sign. I wanted to say, "Thank Him for what? My life is a mess, remember?" But I couldn't. I couldn't deny the evidence that God still loved me. I still had my children, and we had a roof over our heads and food to eat. Despite everything, we were okay. And God was there—I could feel Him. He loved me. He'd never left me, and He never would.

Sobbing, I got down on my knees and thanked God for the beautiful mess my life had become. I thanked Him for His love and His faithfulness to my children and me. But most of all, I thanked Him for a man named Doug, who had become so much more than just my mother's husband. For all his patience and persistence, Doug was now my second dad.

—Diane Stark—

My Prayer

Thank you, Lord, for sending the right people into our lives just when we need them most. Thank you for blessing us with such wonderful friends and family. Help us to encourage and build up one another, especially in times of trouble.
Amen.

| A Change in Perspective

Truth at the Benefit Sale

Hear my prayer, LORD; listen to my cry for mercy.
When I am in distress, I call to you,
because you answer me.
~Psalm 86:6-7

"**C**left lip."

The words had rung in my head since the ultrasound. At twenty-two weeks, a shadow on our unborn child's lip shattered our dreams of the perfect baby. We were facing surgeries, possible feeding problems, and other unknown complications. How were we going to handle this? We prayed every night, desperate for an answer, but the question still haunted us. After two weeks of anguish, we needed a break.

That's why Julia suggested we go to this benefit sale. It was for a six-month-old boy born with a hole in his heart, and as helpless as we felt, we still wanted to help someone else.

We started at opposite ends of the driveway, sorting through tables crowded with clothes and toys. As we met in the middle, Julia picked up a puppet. "Isn't this cute?"

"Do we need another animal?" We own a lot of stuffed animals.

"It's a puppet. We only have a few puppets."

"Well, we're gonna buy something, and he is adorable."

We handed the puppet to the woman at the cash table.

"Oh, that's precious." She checked the price. "Two dollars."

Julia handed her a twenty. "Consider the rest a donation."

The woman's eyes filled with tears. "Oh, God bless you. Are you sure you don't want something else?"

We glanced at each other.

"I'll take one more look," Julia said. "We may have missed something."

As she browsed, a man walked up to the table holding a baby clad in a striped blue shirt and denim overalls.

"Somebody wants to say 'hi.'"

The woman took her baby boy into her arms. At that moment, I saw that he had Down syndrome—as if dealing with heart surgeries wasn't enough.

Julia returned to the cash table with a baby blanket in time for introductions.

"Hi, Noah," we said.

He replied with a glimmering, cherubic smile.

"He's got such an incredible spirit given everything he's been through."

His mother lifted his shirt, revealing a jagged scar that ran like a fault line from his neck to his navel. He giggled as she tickled him, which made us all laugh.

She pulled his shirt back down and cradled him on her shoulder. "It's been harder on us, watching him go through two surgeries and knowing he's got more ahead of him."

I couldn't imagine what she and her husband were going through. I thought about our baby's cleft surgery. It didn't seem as overwhelming anymore.

As we drove away, I could tell that Julia felt as hopeful as I did. Neither of us spoke for several minutes. We each knew what the other was thinking, but Julia put it into words: "With God's help, we can handle this, too."

— David Ozab —

My Prayer

God, our Father, you are always with us, even at our darkest moments, and you answer our prayers in ways we never expect. Hear us now, we beseech you, and give us the help we need to bear the trials of our earthly pilgrimage. This we ask through Jesus Christ our Lord.
Amen.

58

Cakes for My King

Therefore I glory in Christ Jesus
in my service to God.
~Romans 15:17

I sat on the hard pew trying to concentrate on the minister's droning voice. My throat hurt, my body ached, and I was sure if I'd peered in the mirror that I'd see a washed-out complexion. My thoughts proved correct as a concerned friend whispered in my ear, "Are you okay? You're as white as the flour you cook with." I merely shrugged, allowing her words to stroke the self-pity wallowing inside my soul. I closed my eyes, wishing I'd stayed home in bed.

For several weeks, I'd been working as a pastry chef in a new business. The owner's grand plan included a cafe, restaurant, function centre, and hotel all rolled into one. And baking sweet creations for them appeared to be a grand adventure. I bounced with excitement the day I heard they wanted me to come. But five minutes after walking through the door, disappointment arrived with a silent thud. I walked into chaos—an undertrained, skeleton staff and a filthy, grease-encrusted kitchen greeted me.

"It will improve with time," I told myself. I rolled up my sleeves and started scrubbing the kitchen. "After all, it is a new business. Of course, it will be hard work initially."

I went the extra mile by working ten-hour days, six days a week, but bedlam reigned, and my passion for cakes became a burden resulting in burnout.

But God had led me there. I'd felt sure of it... until now. Did I make a mistake? I wanted to throw down my wooden spoon and quit. With a sigh, I slouched into the angular pew. I would quit. I couldn't be expected to work under these conditions.

"... Brother Lawrence worked in a monastery kitchen in the seventeenth century."

My eyes sprung open as the minister's voice penetrated my brain.

"His work was tedious—peeling potatoes and washing dishes."

I stared at the balding reverend.

"Revelation came to Brother Lawrence that everything he did should be done for the glory of God. Going about mundane tasks, he'd murmur, 'I put my little egg-cake into the frying pan for the love of God'" (from *The Practice of the Presence of God*).

The words speared my heart.

In that moment, I decided to persevere. The next day, as I whisked, stirred and baked, I continually muttered, "I put my little egg-cake into the frying pan..."

Crazy days tainted with exhaustion continued, but my attitude slowly changed. When self-pity came knocking, I'd picture that egg-cake sizzling in the pan. Then I told God my work was for Him. Eventually, as the business settled into normalcy, I made a discovery: I no longer concocted cakes with owners, customers or profit in mind. I baked cakes as if baking them for my King.

— Sally Dixon —

My Prayer

Heavenly Father, show me the path to walk. When circumstances get tough, help me to persevere and find strength in you. May the gifts of my hands always bring you glory.
Amen.

59

Letting Go of the Grapes

Therefore encourage one another and build each other up, just as in fact you are doing.
~I Thessalonians 5:11

My husband and I sat on the back patio. The air hung August-hot. I held my iced tea glass against my neck. The cubes had melted, but the glass was still cool.

"It's nice," my husband Lonny said, "to sit for a minute."

He looked toward our aboveground pool. Our five sons splashed and shouted.

"It is," I said. "Here. Have some fruit."

I'd made a big platter for the kids. There were strawberries. Sliced kiwi. Chunks of pineapple. And clusters of crisp, cold grapes.

"Thanks," he said.

I admired his strong jaw. His blue eyes. The way the sun had warmed his skin. Life was good. Sitting here. With him. In the August heat. Listening to the play of our offspring with the only man I've loved.

Lonny grabbed a bunch of purple grapes.

And I cringed.

Lonny has a way of eating grapes. I'm not sure why, but if they're crisp, the sound just echoes in his head. It's loud. It's crunchy. He's not smacking. His mouth is closed. He's polite. But the sound is unnerving. It grates at me. It grates my nerves raw until all I see is red.

Lonny smiled. "Love you," he said, oblivious to the racket that resounded from his head. He reached for another bunch of grapes. Popped one in his mouth. The snapping and popping and chewing began.

I opened my mouth to say something about whatever wild thing happened in his head with the grapes.

But he smiled again. And I looked at my man. My good man. My take-care-of-the-family man. My thoughtful, honest, strong, love-the-Lord man. And the grape sound paled against his goodness.

"I love you, too," I said.

And I meant it.

Sometimes loving means letting go. Letting go of criticism. And letting go of the grapes.

— Shawnelle Eliasen —

My Prayer

Lord, soften my heart to allow your Holy Spirit to enter my soul when unkind words threaten my lips. Help me to use only words that build people up and create an everlasting bond between us.
Amen.

60

Everyday Mundane Things

Trust in the Lord with all your heart and lean not on your own understanding; in all your ways submit to him, and he will make your paths straight.
~*Proverbs 3:5-6*

I t was a typical Bible study evening when we would all gather together to learn more about God and how He loves us. Before the guests arrived at our house, I was trying hard to get into the right frame of mind to worship Him, but my heart was beating fast, spit-up was on my shirt, and I was in a light sweat from preparing to host our small group. My husband and I had just accomplished preparing and eating dinner, picking up toys, doing dishes, bathing our three kids, and getting them all to bed before our first guest arrived at 7:30 P.M.... AND, I MIGHT ADD, IN TWENTY MINUTES FLAT!

During our prayer time in the living room, I listened to the other women share with us about their struggles, hurts, and convictions. One woman was afflicted with a serious illness. Another was going through a divorce. A few had relationship woes. And a young woman was dealing with fertility issues. Again, my heart raced, but this time it was because I felt like I had nothing to share.

What was on my mind? Well, my two-year-old son cried off and on all day, and had a tantrum in the middle of a busy street as we were walking my daughter to preschool. My four-year-old daughter continually tested her limits in her obedience to me as a parent, in play with her brother, and in her speech. My ten-month-old had his fourth ear infection and had thrown up all over me several times that day. Who wanted to hear about my day?

I began to cry when my time came to share because my woes seemed so insignificant compared to the other women in my group. Honestly, I was struggling physically and emotionally as a parent and needed encouragement and prayer from my group. I was exhausted and needed the help of my Savior to get me through. I was quickly reminded by these dear women that the "mountain" I was climbing was just as important as what they were going through.

We often forget to call upon the Lord to help us get through the day, even when it is dealing with a temper tantrum, a growing four-year-old who is testing her independence, or a sick child. It was a wake-up call for me to remember that I don't have to be going through a major life crisis to ask the Lord for strength and perseverance in the everyday mundane things. God can do all things... even stop a temper tantrum mid-throw!

— Elizabeth Fenn —

My Prayer

Dear Heavenly Father, being a parent is a tough job. I want to raise my children in a way that honors and glorifies you. Please remind me to talk to you and ask for strength and wisdom in the simple things I do as I care for them. They are so precious, and we know that every good and perfect gift comes from you! Amen.

61

The Times of Our Lives

*Joy is gone from our hearts; our dancing
has turned to mourning.*
~*Lamentations 5:15*

D uring my ninth week-long trip to Aruba with my husband, we spent our time relaxing under a tree and swimming at the beach during the day, and then sharing exquisite dinners and romantic walks in the evenings. We didn't take any photos because we had visited the island many times before and already had plenty of pictures. On our way to the airport we joked that, other than our tanned skin, we had no proof that we had traveled there!

As we stood in line at check-in, we noticed a family who had been on our chartered plane ride down the week before. This day, however, they all had swollen and tear-filled eyes. Sniffling, they shared only an occasional whispered comment. On the plane, we sat directly behind them: a mother and her four children, ages 8 to 16, with no dad in attendance. We learned that the father had been killed in a jet-skiing accident that week, and his wife and children had to bravely make their way home without him.

We watched the moods of the children go from seemingly carefree while playing cards to quiet sobbing when idle, but the mother's face was chilling. Between hopping seats in an effort to attend to her devastated children, she would sit and stare down at her lap, unable to comprehend what had happened. We could almost feel her pain as we realized that this could have happened to any of us that week. While we were laughing and playing in the water, eating chocolate desserts to our heart's content, this poor family had been experiencing the tragedy of their lives. The vacation they had dreamed about had turned into a nightmare they would never forget. Their photographs would capture indelible moments that would haunt them forever.

I suddenly regretted that we had no pictures from this vacation together. I wondered if the memorialization of events in our minds is only triggered by traumatic events. I closed my eyes and scanned my memory, hoping that my mind had properly registered all the wonderful moments I had shared with my husband that week.

Throughout our lives, our hearts will begin to show the wear and tear from the inevitable misfortunes that befall us. We must consciously stop time and record with our minds those moments that make our hearts swell with love and gratitude—the intimate moments, the surprises, the hours spent with loved ones and friends... *all* the times of our lives.

—Audrey Valeriani —

My Prayer

Dear Father, please help us to remember to cherish the good times of our lives, lest we forget them in the midst of the storms that will surely come. We know that you are with us in times of sorrow and joy. May we see the beauty in the moments we spend with our families and loved.
Amen.

62

Second Best

There is no fear in love. But perfect love drives out fear...
~1 John 4:18

The cheerful new mug welcomed me as I poured my morning coffee. I hoped that my "happy mug," with its hand-painted red, blue and yellow flowers and red handle, would lift me from my depression.

My husband Chuck walked into the kitchen, noticed the mug and frowned. I thought his reaction was to the smell of coffee, which he doesn't like, until he asked about the mug.

"Is that new?"

"Yes! It's my happy mug!" I held it up for him to view.

"Why did you buy another cup when we have so many dishes already?"

My mood crashed as I replied, "Because it's mine."

I fought back tears as he looked at me, bewildered. He shook his head, and then abandoned the subject as he poured his cereal. I knew his thrifty personality didn't comprehend the purchase. He didn't understand my motivation, and I couldn't explain it to him.

True, we had plenty of dishes. When we decided to get married a few months before, we had chosen which possessions we would keep from our previous marriages. We kept his blue-flowered white china, and we'd given away my dishes. It wasn't that I disliked his dishes. It was just that they were a reminder to me of his first marriage that ended when his first wife died, unlike my marriage that had ended by divorce.

We also kept his dining room and living room furniture. Although it was a mutual, rational decision, I began to feel overwhelmed by the reminders that I wasn't Chuck's first choice, despite the fact that we had bought a new home together. I loved our home—exactly what we both wanted in the neighborhood we desired. But a nagging feeling kept reminding me I wasn't his first choice, and that I'd never measure up to his first wife.

I knew I shouldn't feel that way, but I was afraid to tell Chuck what was bothering me. So I bought a new mug just to have something that was mine, not "theirs."

Yet it hadn't worked. I was running away from the problem, avoiding even the mention of her name, afraid it would make both of us uncomfortable. Finally, I decided to face my fear.

That evening, I surprised Chuck by asking him to tell me about his first wife and how they met. As I asked more questions and listened, a mental picture of the young couple formed in my mind.

He stopped, watching my response. "What else do you want to know?"

"Tell me about her illness."

With tears in his eyes, he told about the four-year battle with cancer. His pain became my pain as I listened. The barrier was down. The fear was gone. We both breathed a sigh of relief and embraced.

The next morning as I entered the kitchen, I smiled at the sunshine-yellow walls Chuck had painted for me with the white beadboard he had installed below. Looking up, I saw the painting we'd bought on our honeymoon. All around me was evidence of Chuck's love for me and our life together.

Chuck entered the room, and I said, "I need to tell you something."

"Okay." He looked worried.

With a smile, I said, "I wish I could thank Joan, because she helped you to be the man you are now."

He nodded. "You're right. She did." He leaned over and kissed me. "I love you."

"I know," I replied.

—Marilyn Turk—

My Prayer

Dear Father, you truly know all the healing that we need in our lives. Thank you, God, for staying by our sides whenever tensions arise. How blessed we are in knowing that your presence always surrounds us.
Amen.

63

Romance Shmo-mance

Nehemiah said, "Go and enjoy choice food and sweet drinks, and send some to those who have nothing prepared. This day is holy to our Lord. Do not grieve, for the joy of the LORD is your strength."
~Nehemiah 8:10

H ere it is again—Valentine's Day. For couples, it can be a wonderful day, but for singles, not so much. It can be downright dismal.

As a divorced mother, I learned years ago to make plans for myself on special days like Christmas and my birthday. It kept me from falling into the holiday blues like so many singles do. But while my son was growing up, Valentine's Day didn't bother me much. Back then, it was mostly about buying something fun for him, helping him address valentines for his classmates, and making cupcakes to take to his school party.

Now, my son is twenty-seven and no longer at home. I've been single for twenty-five years, and the February focus on love and romance is really starting to bug me. A lot. I sneer at the commercials depicting a handsome husband surprising his wife with diamonds. I cringe at the silly sitcoms suggesting that anyone without a date on Valentine's Day must be a hairy ape. And as for those endless store displays of mushy cards, heart-shaped boxes of chocolates, and bouquets of roses… more than once I've contemplated mowing them down with my grocery cart. Accidentally, of course.

Yesterday, as I stood in line behind a young man who was buying one of those Valentine's bouquets, I thought to myself, "I can't wait till February fifteenth." Then a guy behind me leaned forward and asked the young man how much the roses cost. He wanted to buy some for his own wife. I smiled and said, "Smart husbands do things like that. You must be a smart husband." He sheepishly told me that it had taken him a while to learn to be "a smart husband."

As I thought about that, it brightened my spirits to think of this guy making his wife happy by presenting her with Valentine's flowers. That gave me an idea. Rather than getting depressed because I would not be getting roses or chocolate or diamonds or even a kiss, I decided to take the focus off myself by thinking of someone else with the same need. Immediately, I thought of three women in my church. They are lovely, godly women, but none of them has ever married. Like me, they would not be getting Valentine's gifts.

I went back into the store and bought four small, heart-shaped boxes of chocolates. Then I arranged to deliver them to my friends secretly. The fourth box, of course, was for me. No, it isn't the same as getting chocolate from a loving husband. But maybe, just for a moment, I brightened their spirits on Valentine's Day. It sure lifted mine.

— Teresa Ambord —

My Prayer

Heavenly Father, help me to remember that my strength comes from your joy, not my circumstances. Please make me aware of the needs of those around me and show me a way to help.
Amen.

64

Lessons from Matt

"The King will reply, 'Truly I tell you, whatever you did for one of the least of these brothers and sisters of mine, you did for me.'"
~Matthew 25:40

"**J**ust what am I doing in a place like this?" I had turned down this job assignment two years before, but now it was this job, as an aide in the school for the severe and profoundly disabled, or no job. This was the oldest building in the district. The walls reeked with fifty years of sweat, vomit, and vermin odor. It had been one of the city's most beautiful facilities; now it warehoused those whom some administrators wanted out of sight and out of mind.

The small bathroom smelled of urine and human waste. The hard tile floor cut into my knees. I slung the jeans I had just pulled off the thin, braced legs of my nine-year-old charge and grumbled aloud.

"I wanted to write songs and stories for you, God."

I had spent most of my three weeks at this job with Matt, trying to get him to go to the bathroom on the potty, put a block in a can or at least make eye contact. To get him to look me in the eyes proved to be the most difficult. His eyes seemed to be the only thing he was able to control. He had no verbal skills, little motor control. All he had was the ability to look away or squeeze his eyes shut, anything but eye contact.

As I took the soiled underwear off Matt to clean his legs and bottom, I dropped the feces-covered underwear on my dress. "Oh, Matt, look what you've done!" I screamed.

He gave his soundless laugh and smiled a grin made toothless from the many falls his wobbly legs had taken. Most days that smile would have melted my heart, but not today. My love was stretched thin, and my patience broke. "God, I hate this."

The small room grew still, and I felt Matt's stare. I glanced up and met his eyes. Large and luminous, they looked into mine, staring into my soul. In the quietness of the moment, I heard words with my heart—not Matt's voice and not mine.

"I didn't ask you to rewrite Sunday school literature. I didn't ask you to write songs. I said if you do it unto the least of these, you've done it unto me." Then Matt looked away.

God spoke to my heart in a most profound way in that smelly bathroom. In the years that followed, I learned to listen, and Matt taught me so many things. You don't have to be capable of seesawing to sit on one and enjoy white clouds in a blue sky. Soundless laughter and silent tears often communicate better than words. Life in its most simple form is sometimes life at its best. Probably the best lesson I learned: God talks the loudest through the weakest.

— Peggy Purser Freeman —

My Prayer

Father God, thank you for allowing us to meet your needs by doing for others. Forgive us for not seeing immediately the plans you have for us—even when the plans are not those we would choose. Help us to listen and to search for you in all situations.
Thank you for the people in our life who become great teachers.
Amen.

65

A Shift in Focus

But when you give to the needy, do not let your left hand know what your right hand is doing, so that your giving may be in secret. Then your Father, who sees what is done in secret, will reward you.
~Matthew 6:3-4

I am a breast cancer survivor, and my husband Brad and I were in Houston for some annual tests. We went to a cute little village to waste some time between appointments. Brad and I sat on a bench, and I quickly noticed a man on the bench across from us. By his appearance, I soon gathered that he was homeless. He also seemed to be mentally ill as he was having a conversation with himself.

I leaned over to my husband and said, "Please ask this man if we could buy him lunch."

I could tell Brad was a little hesitant to approach the man, who was filthy, and had huge holes in his jeans and sores on his lips. Nonetheless, Brad went up and asked him, "Can I buy you a sandwich?"

The man answered, "Yeah, yeah," so Brad went into the sandwich shop while I stayed outside.

I tried to put himself in this man's place. Young moms walked by with their children. Other people were talking on their cell phones, holding bags full of purchased items. No one paid any attention to this man.

After a bit, Brad came out with a full meal, which we handed to the man. Then I said to Brad, "Ask him what size pants he wears."

Brad looked surprised, but quickly realized where I was going with this. We buzzed to the Gap to buy an outfit.

When we showed the man the things we had bought for him, he looked into our eyes and said, "Oh, yeah? For me? Great, thank you."

Then he reached out and shook Brad's hand. Their eyes met, and there was so much love in that moment that you could feel the connection between them. Later, as Brad and I sat in our car, I saw that my husband was crying.

I realized that the Lord had sent the homeless man on the bench. Focused on someone else, thinking about another's situation, I quickly forgot about my own worries. As I waited to get the results of my MRI, the Lord taught me how powerful it is to focus on other things. When you are in a time full of worries and anxiety, ask the Lord to give you something else to think about. Maybe, just maybe, He has someone in mind for you.

— Kim Leonard —

My Prayer

Dearest Father in Heaven, some days I feel that I am in a rush, thinking of my own thoughts and needs. I pray that today you will use me in your service to others. Help me reach out to others and show them that they are not alone in this great world. Let my actions remind them of your love each and every day.
Amen.

66

A Cure for the Worry Gene

I will not leave you as orphans; I will come to you.
~John 14:18

"I found a beautiful place to sit outside and study. It's grassy, beside a small pond, and has several huge shade trees."

My daughter, Mallory, was describing to me over her cell phone a special spot she had discovered at the university she is attending. As she explained the spot in detail, I envisioned it as a lovely place.

"And, Mom, it's so quiet. Secluded behind two classroom buildings, hardly anyone comes around, and..."

What? Wait a minute! Secluded? No one around? Suddenly, I was envisioning something totally different and much more sinister. My *"what if gene"* kicked into high gear. *What if* a deranged person attacked her in this secluded place? *What if* a hungry gator was lurking in that pond? *What if* she needed help and no one was within hearing distance?

Why do I naturally "go there" with all these worries and doubts? I must have inherited this worry gene from my father. In any stressful situation, my mother remained relatively calm while my father thought of all the horrible scenarios that might happen. And although I do believe that being cautious can prevent many ills, I also realize that long-term worrying can be as destructive as any human disease. It affects not only the worriers of the world, but all the folks who love them. Where is the dividing line between being a cautious, caring parent and teaching your kids that the world is a scary place to live?

Jesus was direct in his command for us not to worry. "Therefore do not worry about tomorrow, for tomorrow will worry about itself" (Matthew 6:34).

I am learning to use Jesus's words to fight my worry gene. Now, in any given situation, I instruct or advise my teenagers on what I feel to be the best course of action, and then I thank God for taking care of them, especially while they are living away from home. I ask God to watch over them and envision His protective arms wrapped around them. Then, and only then, can I let go. By overcoming my anxiety through prayer and faith, I spend less time fretting and more time enjoying what God has so graciously given me.

— Deborah R. Albeck —

My Prayer

Dear Heavenly Father, thank you for caring for my children throughout the years. Please continue to wrap your loving, protective arms around them as they live out their lives more and more independently of me. In Jesus Christ's most precious name, I pray.
Amen.

67

Just Muddle Through

It is God who arms me with strength and keeps my way secure.

~2 Samuel 22:33

When my husband began a new job and we moved to a different city, our family's life changed drastically. Uneasy about his new job, my husband worked long hours. When he was home, he became withdrawn and depressed. Our kids grumbled about leaving their friends and rebelled about attending a new school. To add to the problems, our teenage daughter developed a physical problem requiring hospitalization and surgery in a city sixty miles away. I found myself torn between caring for our daughter, trying to find ways to help our boys adjust, and coping with my husband's discontent.

While our daughter recovered in the hospital, I stayed nearby with an elderly friend who possessed a strong Christian faith. I respected her wisdom and hoped she might have a solution for my turmoil. Ready to crack with frustration, worried sick about my family, and feeling like a total failure as a wife and mother, I blubbered to Carolyn, "What should I do? How can I help my family survive this mess?"

Carolyn did not hesitate to answer, but her advice shocked me.

"Well," she said, "pray a lot and just muddle through." Could the answer to my worries be that simple?

As I contemplated her answer, a new realization hit me. In my arrogance, I had thought I could solve everyone's problems. As a caring wife and mother, I felt I should know all the answers and somehow magically make everything okay. I wrestled with guilt because I had not been able to create happiness and contentment for everyone. Carolyn's answer helped me recognize I was not a perfect person capable of making life smooth for all my loved ones. Sometimes that is not possible.

I did what my friend suggested. I turned my struggles over to God in prayer, and I muddled through. As a family, we eventually survived the adjustments that came with the move, and in time our daughter got well. Our family still experienced some rough times, but we managed.

Now I know it is not my responsibility to fix all the problems and make everyone happy all the time. I will always try my best to be a good wife and mother, but many days all I can do is pray a lot and just muddle through. God understands our limitations.

— Barbara Brady —

My Prayer

Dear Lord, I find myself struggling with the need
for perfection in my life. Help me to turn my
struggles over to you in prayer.
With your guidance, I can become the
person you created me.
Amen.

68

Worry or Pray

Cast all your anxiety on him because he cares for you.
~1 Peter 5:7

My little boy sat all alone in one corner of the pre-K class-room. His red-rimmed eyes and swollen nose told the story of his day at school—another day spent in tears.

Too young to write words, he was making pictures of everything he'd done that day. When a teacher attempted to throw away some of his many scribbled papers, he cried, "No, don't take them! I might forget to tell Mommy and Daddy about something I did today."

A bell halted the frenzy of crayon on paper. In moments, he'd have to put on his coat to go out for recess, but suddenly he couldn't resist an urge to tap his cheek and count the repetitions. His stomach ached, and he wanted to go home. He'd skipped lunch when he saw the broken crackers on the tray—evidence to him that someone might have taken a bite from his lunch.

When the three o'clock bell rang, he tried to remember how to pack his backpack in the exact order he did yesterday and the day before that. Perhaps that would make everything all right.

At home, this inner conflict continued. He hardly touched his supper. "See these animal shapes in the chicken, Mom? I can't eat those."

"Try this then." I pointed at his macaroni and cheese.

"Are there germs in it?"

After supper, he played with his toys, but used only his smallest finger to touch them. The rest of his hand coiled in a tight fist. That week, the preschool teacher called me, concerned about his actions at school. I wasn't sure what was happening, but I knew we needed to see our pediatrician.

When Austin was diagnosed with obsessive compulsive disorder at age five, I had so many questions. Did I do something to cause this? Would he ever be "normal?" Why us? It broke my heart to see a little boy with so much anxiety. It hurt my pride that I couldn't make it better.

Austin was placed on medication, and we saw a therapist who taught him how to "boss back the worries" when they came. During one of those sessions, the doctor asked him, "What should we do when we have worries?"

"We pray and ask Jesus to take them away."

I grinned. I'm sure the therapist expected Austin to respond with one of the techniques he'd learned, but in simple understanding he demonstrated that we should turn to Jesus first. His faith inspired me and reminded me that God was present, even in the counseling room.

Scripture tells us to have faith like a child. Think about that. A child believes that God can do anything. In simple faith, Austin demonstrated the principle from 1 Peter 5:7—to cast all our anxiety on God because He cares for us. It's so easy for moms to worry. We have plenty to worry about! But God asks us to give it to Him because He loves us and is able to bear our burdens.

By the end of second grade, Austin was off all medication, and he hasn't seen a therapist in more than seven years. I praise God for healing him, and I'm so grateful for what I learned in the process. God can handle my worries. He can handle yours, too.

— Michelle Rayburn —

My Prayer

Sovereign God, help me to let go of my anxiety and rest in your ability to see the road ahead. Thank you for loving me and caring for my every need. Teach me how to be an example of faith to my children as I trust in you.

Amen.

69

The Cross by the Side of the Road

But let all who take refuge in you be glad;
let them ever sing for joy. Spread your
protection over them, that those who love
your name may rejoice in you. For surely,
O Lord, you bless the righteous; you
surround them with your favor
as with a shield.

~Psalm 5:11-12

Every day when I drove my second-born son to middle school, I noticed a little wooden cross by the side of the road. The shoelaces on a worn pair of athletic shoes had been tied together and draped over the top of the cross. A weathered bouquet of plastic flowers lay at the base. It marked the site where a fourteen-year-old boy had been killed by a car as he crossed the street on his bicycle.

Tears would fill my eyes as I passed it because the boy was the same age as my oldest son. I couldn't help but think, "If it can happen to that child, it could happen to my own." I would think about how his family only had memories now of their beloved son and how their hearts must be aching.

My oldest son is now nineteen and in college, but I am still haunted by the boy on the bicycle. When my son is out late with his friends, I listen to storms raging outside and pray that he makes it home safely. Surely, the storm in my heart is just as fierce. I stay awake until I hear the door open and know that he is well. And I utter a prayer of thanksgiving that we both made it through the storm.

As the mother of four sons in a scary world, I know that I'll never completely stop worrying. But I know I need to try. When I worry so much about my children, I not only make myself miserable, but I hurt God with my lack of trust in Him. I want to pull my sons close and never let them out of my sight, but I know I can't protect them forever. I have to let go and let God be their protector.

—Susan M. Heim—

My Prayer

God, please extend your loving protection to my children. Help me to allow them their freedom and to trust that you will care for them at all times. For I know you are the ultimate parent, dear Father, and you love my children as much as I do. Amen.

70

Consider the Daisies

"If that is how God clothes the grass of the field, which is here today and tomorrow is thrown into the fire, will he not much more clothe you—you of little faith?"
~Matthew 6:30

"We'll be okay, honey," my brightest voice mustered. In reality, my heart was heavy.

My husband, Jesse, a state government worker, called to break the news of a proposal for twelve unpaid furlough days for the next year. We had already endured the effects of six furlough days.

Jesse and I had become a one-income family in 2006 so that I could care for our newborn son, Andrew. Our nation's economic meltdown followed our decision. Grocery expenses rose, and gas prices skyrocketed while we lived on a less-than-average income. But we were thrifty and continually hopeful, and we had another child, our daughter, Gracie. For four years, God's provisions amazed me. Now, as we anticipated lost income, doubt chipped away at my faith.

At the same time, a drought plagued us. Though I watered faithfully, my petunias and Gerber daisies sagged like my forlorn spirit. After weeks, the rain came. Since summer had slipped into autumn, the downpour seemed inconsequential.

"Let's go for a walk, Mama!" Andrew exclaimed the next day, after the storm had cleared. Why not? I thought to myself. It was uncharacteristically warm, and a walk might help me feel better.

I ambled along in the sun's warmth, pushing Gracie in her stroller and watching Andrew pump his legs up and down on his Spiderman bike. Just ahead of me, Andrew put on his brakes, jumped off, and crouched down beside a patch of grass.

"Look, Mama, daisies!" Andrew shouted, amazed. I looked down where Andrew pointed and, sure enough, there was a beautiful patch of daisies. We hadn't noticed them before, even though we walked past this grass almost every day. Although all the other wildflowers had long succumbed to the parched landscape, the vibrant daisies flourished.

"How did they get there?" Andrew asked, as perplexed as I was.

I thought of "Consider the Lilies." The simple message in scripture and the beautiful song tell us that if God cares for the birds, flowers, and grass, He will care for us, too. My worries dissipated, and a slow smile formed on my face. For the first time in weeks, a new spark of hope flickered in my heart.

"Sometimes, it takes a little rain to breathe new life into something," I replied to my son's question.

And sometimes it takes a walk on an uncharacteristically warm day and a thriving patch of wild daisies to breathe new life into a doubting heart. That day, God reminded me once again that He cares for the lilies of the field, the daisies on the roadside—and my family and me.

— Janeen Lewis —

My Prayer

Dear Father, thank you for blessings that abound even in times of drought. When my soul grows weary with the worries of this world, you continually renew it with a fresh perspective. Amen.

71

From Chaos to Restoration

Then Jacob made a vow, saying, "If God will be with me and will watch over me on this journey I am taking and will give me food to eat and clothes to wear so that I return safely to my father's household, then the LORD will be my God..."
~Genesis 28:20-21

While studying simplicity, our women's Bible study instructor asked us to determine our individual focus. I laughed outright. Focusing—on anything—was impossible.

In October, my husband, Chris, left a secure job for self-employment, but ensuring the company's success meant grueling work hours, and my younger son and I rarely saw him. He seemed oblivious to the destruction his obsessive behavior wreaked on our marriage and family. Work and success had replaced us, and the rejection felt final. Then my father died, and Christmas was marred by grief. My younger craved his dad's presence; my older son struggled uncharacteristically in college. In April, I battled injuries from a car accident and a hostile insurance company. Finances were shaky, and my marriage hung by a thread. One word summed up my life: chaos.

We'd weathered rough times before in our twenty-seven-year marriage, including our daughter's death, and God had shepherded us through every inch of life's difficulties. Yet now everything seemed to be unraveling. I was at the end of my coping rope, directionless and hopeless.

The one flickering light at the end of the tunnel was our upcoming vacation, but as the departure date neared, the business was at a critical, sink-or-swim juncture. Yet in my mind, this trip had been our last resort, a Hail Mary to save us. What should I do now?

No sooner had I cried out the question than God gave me an answer: go alone. Drive up the California coast? Alone? Having buried my own dreams for so long, I no longer knew my capabilities.

Go alone. It seemed as though God was giving me permission to cease striving and pleasing, to come away with Him. He seemed to say, "Let me take care of you, and everything else." So, I stepped out in faith.

I discarded electronic devices and rejected guilt. I feasted on sunsets, seashores and vistas. I saturated myself with God. I prayed and really listened to Him. As I journeyed, stress dropped like scales from my soul.

And my eyes were opened to how I'd contributed to my marriage's decline. I'd become weak and needy, unfairly expecting Chris to be everything to me. I helped too much, pushed too much, expected too much, enabled too much. I needed to get out of the way and let God work on Chris, so he could grow and become the man he was created to be. As clarity brightened the future, my spirit rejoiced.

Four days before the trip ended, Chris joined me. When I saw him standing curbside at the airport—duffle bag in hand, hopeful, expectant smile on his face—I knew my prayers were answered. Our three-day reunion was honeymoon-like. I shared with Chris everything I'd learned and asked for his forgiveness. Chris apologized for everything he'd done to the family.

Redeemed and restored, our future once again glowed with hope and purpose. I'd trusted God and taken a risk. He'd rewarded us with a miracle.

— Andrea Arthur Owan —

My Prayer

Thank you, God, for answering when we call, for providing a way out when the road in front of us looks bleak and hopeless or too steep for us to climb. Remind us that often all we need to do is come away with you to listen and rest, and that risks orchestrated by you are worth taking. Amen.

72

Beating the
Bed Rest Blues

*A woman giving birth to a child has pain because
her time has come; but when her baby is born she
forgets the anguish because of her joy that a
child is born into the world.*

~John 16:21

It was time for my first ultrasound, and I nervously awaited the results. My OB/GYN pulled up the monitor, and I searched the screen for any recognizable picture. There on the screen was a little beating heart. I was overjoyed. As he moved the wand over my rather pregnant belly, he found just what he was looking for: a second heartbeat. It was the first confirmation that my husband and I were to have twins. Not one little bundle to care for, but two. Was I nervous? Was I excited? Was I surprised? Of course, I was all of these and more.

The pregnancy continued, and I experienced the common multiple pregnancy problem of terrible morning sickness. Around the 17th week, I had my first scare when I started bleeding. The doctors put me in the hospital to monitor the situation. I remember praying to

God to protect these two beautiful souls inside my body. I waited out the night and, fortunately, the bleeding stopped. They released me the next day, but fear had taken a place in my heart.

It seemed like most of my doctor's visits were checkups to see if anything was wrong. Looking back on them now, I see that I was in such a fearful place. Did I feel an early contraction? Were the babies growing at the correct rate? All these questions and more percolated in my mind.

Being on bed rest in any multiple pregnancy is almost a given, and I was no exception. When the doctor put me on partial bed rest around week 28, I thought he was kidding. I had a two-year-old to care for. My husband was traveling quite a bit. Who was going to care for my daughter, Kara? I tried to stay off my feet, but I was feeling invincible. Staying on the couch for four to six hours a day while caring for a young toddler was not feasible. So I did too much, and I paid for it later.

When I was admitted to the hospital for full bed rest, it finally hit me. I had to slow down and protect these precious bundles inside me. My only job at that point was to keep them inside until week 35 or later. Lying there for two weeks really humbled me. For once in my life, I was dependent on the help of others. I couldn't do it alone anymore. And the amazing thing I realized was that God never expected me to go at it alone. He had back-up help just waiting in the wings all along.

Women from our church sprang into action immediately when my husband announced my hospitalization at prayer time during the service. They signed up to bring meals to the house and even arranged babysitting for my daughter. I received visitors in the hospital, and one lovely person painstakingly tried to show me how to needlepoint. No longer was I fearful. I felt hope because I had God's loving arms wrapped around me.

Reflecting back on it now, God was there each and every step of the way. He had a plan for me to be a mother of twins, and my womb was a place for these dear babies to grow. They needed me just as much as I so desperately needed Him.

In hindsight, I wish that I had given my worries to God much earlier. But, with God's help and the gift of friendship from others, I made it to 36½ weeks before delivering. Our twins were born healthy and ready to take on the world—and our life.

—Karen Talcott—

My Prayer

Dear Lord, thank you for the loving care that you always provide for me. I feel so blessed that I am part of a church family that steps into action when someone is in need.
Amen.

73

The Envelope

He replied, "Because you have so little faith. Truly I tell you, if you have faith as small as a mustard seed, you can say to this mountain, 'Move from here to there,' and it will move. Nothing will be impossible for you."
~Matthew 17:20

My dream of motherhood seemed to be disappearing. After the tenth negative pregnancy test in less than five years, I had given up hope of ever being called "Mom." My husband and I were surrounded by pregnant family and friends. We loved them all, but it was a constant reminder of the loss we were feeling.

"Don't you love us anymore?" I asked God one morning. "I don't understand why I'm not pregnant yet." The pain seemed more than I could bear.

One afternoon, a friend came by my house. We'd known each other since college, and I knew she cared about my pain.

"I believe God will answer your prayers in an amazing way," she said.

I burst into tears, wanting to believe her.

"What will your first child's name be?" she asked.

"Michael or Michelle," I answered. Richard and I had chosen the names long ago, before we married.

She wrote something on a piece of paper, folded it, and put it in an envelope. "Open this when he or she arrives."

I put the envelope in a pocket of my purse, figuring I would never have the opportunity to read what was inside.

"Have faith," she said before she left.

Five years went by, and Richard and I still longed for a child. Then, one morning, a friend called to tell us about the classes she and her husband were taking to be eligible for adoption through the state. We signed up right away.

Seven months later, we'd been approved, having completed our parenting classes, home studies, and paperwork. It was time to wait again, but this time there was hope.

And on November 2, 1992, the call came. We had been accepted for adoption of a nine-month-old girl. Her foster parents named her Michelle.

God had answered our long hours of prayer. It hadn't been the way I'd expected, but the results were all that I had dreamed. My daughter is the joy of my life.

It wasn't until nearly a year later, cleaning out my closet, that I found an old purse. I rummaged through it as my daughter played around my feet. In a zippered pocket was an envelope. I opened it and found a mustard seed necklace and a folded piece of paper. I read the note my friend had written. "Kathy, give little Michael or Michelle a hug for me. Never give up faith or hope."

I glanced down at Michelle and smiled. She grinned back. "Mama."

My friend had planted seeds of faith in my heart. God had watered them, and my dream came to life and called me Mama.

— Kathryn Lay —

My Prayer

When it seems that all hope is lost, let me remember the sweet and simple words, "God is with me." I thank you for bringing people into my life who help strengthen my faith when it rests on rocky soil. You are the one true Father! In your name…
Amen.

74

In His Arms

The eternal God is your refuge, and underneath are the everlasting arms.
~Deuteronomy 33:27

"**M**y baby is choking!" my panicked voice cried as I tightly squeezed the nurse's call button. Mesmerized, my husband and I had been gazing at our two-day-old son, Andrew, while he slumbered. Suddenly, he began to kick his legs and spew frothy saliva from his lips. My husband grabbed Andrew to run with him to the nurse's station, but two nurses reacted to my call and met us at our hospital door. Both my husband and a nurse gave Andrew hard pats on the back to stop his choking. He immediately stopped struggling, relaxed, and breathed easily. The mysterious choking was baffling. Nothing was found to be wrong with our healthy, full-term newborn, and we were discharged from the hospital just hours later.

I had given birth to my son two days before, but it was in those few terrifying seconds while he choked that I became a parent. The cocoon of peaceful bliss that surrounded my heart was pierced with worry and fear, and a multitude of questions ricocheted through my mind. What if we hadn't been there when Andrew's episode had started? What if he did it again? From how many other dangers must I protect him?

Our first night home was a sleepless one for me. I stayed up, checking on my son in his crib until, exhausted, I fell asleep on the couch near daybreak, my ear glued to the baby monitor. The next day at Andrew's checkup, I told his doctor that I hadn't slept and why.

"You can't keep doing that," he said of my lack of sleep. He tried to reassure me that Andrew would be all right. But that was hard for me to accept. Andrew was so little and helpless. I had to protect him. I felt the responsibility weigh heavily on my shoulders, and my heart was burdened.

And then some sage words from a mom of three in my Sunday school class came back to me. She had imparted some of her wisdom to me before I started my own journey of motherhood.

"Children are a gift from God," she said. "They do not belong to us; they are entrusted to us by God for a little while."

I thought of Hannah from the Bible. She was able to give her young son, Samuel, back to God at the tabernacle and rejoice. She realized, as did my friend, that children are a gift from the Lord. It was hard for me to accept that ultimately I wasn't the one in control; I can't save Andrew the way God can. As his earthly mother, my responsibility is to teach him that his Heavenly Father is sovereign. Is there any guarantee that he will be safe from all the dangers that sometimes enter my imaginative mind? Not in this imperfect, fallen world. Andrew's spiritual protection is what will matter for eternity, and the only place that security can be found is in the everlasting arms of God. That is where I must place him, along with my worries.

When I turn my fears over to God, I stop turning and tossing at night. Only in His arms can my heart truly be wrapped in a cocoon of blissful peace.

—Janeen Lewis—

My Prayer

Dear God, help me to put my trust in you to protect my child and calm my fears. When my thoughts stray to places of darkness, help me to turn back to your pure light and truth. Thank you for the precious gift of motherhood, and I ask you to grant me the wisdom to be a good mother. Amen.

75

Writing on the Wall

Let love and faithfulness never leave you;
bind them around your neck,
write them on the tablet of your heart.
~Proverbs 3:3

Colorful chalk designs on summer sidewalks had always brought a smile to my face, whether I was the artist or the admirer. But I never expected that finding chalk markings on the interior walls of my house as an adult would have the same result, or that I would be the artist!

Between picking up socks and sweeping away dust bunnies from under my sons' beds, I came across a discarded piece of white chalk. The idea came to me in the instant I touched it, and I pursued it before my mom-mind caught up with me. I took to the walls with that chalk and wrote each of my sons a note, listing some of the many things I love about them.

Satisfied with my work, I headed to my own room to pick up socks and clear out the dust bunnies from under my bed. Upon coming up from under the frame, I came face-to-face with the empty space of blue wall above the bed that my husband and I have been blessed to share for thirteen-some years. The words I had written on my sons' walls rolled through my mind, and a question formed in my heart:

What words would I have for my spouse? I sat on the edge of the bed for a moment and allowed this thought to linger.

Words have always held great value to me. The very words of the promises and love that God has for me have built up my faith and relationship with Him. I began to think of all these promises and gifts of words that have been written on my walls—the walls of my heart. These words were given at times when I needed to recall that I was loved and cared for unconditionally. As a mother, it took little persuasion to give similar words to my little men, but what about my husband? Did I have words to offer to him? Was I willing to give the gift of words to build and form our relationship? Could I write on his wall?

Ignoring the freshly folded sheets and well-placed pillows, I retrieved the chalk, stood on the bed, and began to write words for my spouse. Even after thirteen years of not-always-wedded-bliss, but of real-life love, I offered the very same gift that is constantly bestowed unto me—words of affirmation and love. As I stepped off the bed, and re-adjusted the sheets and pillows, I smiled.

When my husband came home that day, the boys excitedly showed him their messages. As he entered our room to change after his long day of work, I could almost feel the smile on his face as he took in the message written for him on the wall above our bed. Words don't come easily from me in my marriage, but they are worth all the effort. As God continues daily to write His messages of love and affirmation on the walls of my heart, I can continue to pass on messages of love and affirmation on the walls of my spouse's heart in the hope that our relationship will not only represent the one we can have with our Heavenly Father, but so that it can be built upon the foundation of it.

—Angela Wolthuis—

My Prayer

Heavenly Father, thank you for your unconditional love. May we be examples of that love to our families. Please give us the grace, the love, and the words to write those affirmations on the tablets of the hearts of our loved ones.
Amen.

76

Words to Live By

Therefore do not worry about tomorrow,
for tomorrow will worry about itself.
Each day has enough trouble of its own.
~Matthew 6:34

The sun beamed in through the big bay window and masked the dank and dark feeling that only a hospital room can provide. A line of light illuminated my grandfather's face, and for just a moment he closed his eyes as if allowing the warmth of the sun to saturate his entire body. When your life is approaching its end, I imagine all the bitterness subsides, and the jaded moments that we put so much stock in become petty and meaningless.

My grandfather opened his eyes slowly and said, "Don't live your life without living it. I worked too hard. I missed many things because I was trying to make a better tomorrow for my family. What good is a tomorrow if you keep missing today?"

He rolled back over and closed his eyes once more as if allowing what he said to marinate within me. I realized, with the sun basking on his pale and aged face and his eyes closed in deep contemplation, that he was reviewing his life as if he were a bystander. I knew that when my grandfather spoke those words to me, he was feeling regret. Though we cannot change the past, we can influence the future.

I was twenty-two years old—an unstoppable college graduate with the sky as my limit. I knew that my grandfather was bestowing upon me yet another valuable tool to add to my defense against this sometimes harsh world.

That night, I slept the soundest I ever had. A sense of peace and tranquility fell over me that I hadn't felt in a long while. My worries, cares and concerns seemed weightless and were replaced by the almost haunting sound of my grandfather. *"Don't live your life without living it."*

I was abruptly woken out of a sound sleep by my mother. Before she muttered the words through sobs and tears, I knew why she was waking me.

Later that morning as I sat at the kitchen table, a single tear ran down my face. Through the window, a ray of sunlight engulfed my entire body and warmed me from the inside out. I knew it was a hug from my grandfather. And I knew that for the rest of my life his words would reverberate in my thoughts. He had given me the best advice I ever had.

—Christina M. Harris—

My Prayer

Lord, how we lead our life is a gift to you. Our time here on Earth can be short, long, fulfilling, or full of pain and suffering. Remind us each day to live it for you. When we center it on you, all things are possible.

Amen.

77

My Petri Dish Experiment

But the wisdom that comes from heaven is first of all pure; then peace-loving, considerate, submissive, full of mercy and good fruit, impartial and sincere. Peacemakers who sow in peace reap a harvest of righteousness.
~James 3:17-18

I was a stay-at-home mother, and I loved that role. But being a wife, not so much. My husband and I never fought, but we didn't bring much joy to each other either.

While studying the book of James, I was asked to look up the word "peacemaker." I did it half-heartedly because, of course, I already knew what it meant: one who settles conflicts. But the study taught me that a peacemaker also *prevents* conflicts by creating peace in the first place. Wow! Now, that was a different challenge. It required me to monitor the words that came out of my mouth, the tone in which I spoke them, and my actions. I liked the first definition a whole lot better; I was pretty good at that one. I didn't score high on the "creating peace" definition.

My husband and I were leaving for Hawaii, just the two of us. It was the ideal opportunity to monitor everything I said. I called it my "petri dish experiment." A petri dish is used in research laboratories. Often it's filled with a culture medium (Hawaii), contaminated in some way (by my tongue), and then the researcher (me) waits to see what grows.

In Hawaii, I claimed every opportunity to give my husband praise or to thank him. I stopped before speaking to evaluate whether my words were hurtful. I began to recognize how carelessly my words had slipped out in the past, and I was stunned by how easily they could wound instead of encourage. With intentional care, I chose words that exhorted. I discovered, much to my surprise, that I didn't always have to say the first thing that came to my mind. If I paused—and, believe me, that was hard to do—I could determine whether my words were true, necessary, and kind.

This went on for several days. I thought my husband would catch on and ask, "What's up with you?" He's an intelligent man, but he never caught on. By the end of the trip, he couldn't do enough for me. He had us biking down a volcano and snorkeling, two things we'd never done on past visits. I'm an outdoor girl, so he did these things for me.

My carefully chosen words created a miracle before my eyes. My precious husband grew taller. He stood straighter. He shined. My petri dish of praise and exhortation produced a happier husband.

I wish I could look back on that experiment as a complete victory. And to the extent that I learned an important lesson, it was—a big one. But part of the lesson was one of shame and sadness. All those years, all those chances to build him up… what would have happened if I'd done my part better? All I could do about the past was ask for forgiveness and change my ways for the future.

Now, the children are gone and it's just the two of us. We've discovered joy in each other. My petri dish of peace-producing words grew a healthier, happier marriage.

—DV Mason—

My Prayer

Lord, may the words that I speak be chosen by you. Give me, I pray, insight into the effect of my words before I speak them.

Amen.

78

Gossip Hurts

Though you probe my heart and examine me at night, though you test me, you will find nothing, I have resolved that my mouth will not sin.

~Psalm 17:3

Recently, I accepted an invitation to lunch with a group of friends. After the usual greetings and placing our orders, we got down to business. And when I say "business," I really mean "gossip." We shared about our own lives, and then started in on the other friends who were not there. We talked about one friend's divorce and all the dirty details we had heard collectively. How much money was she getting? Did he really cheat on her or was it the other way around? All of it was really none of our business, but our tongues wagged for a couple of hours.

As I drove home, I started to feel the twinges of guilt set in. Had I really said all those mean-spirited things at the table? I certainly had been active in the discussions, so I couldn't say that I was an innocent bystander. And the more I thought of my behavior, the more I wanted to hang my head in shame.

I try so hard to remain a Godly person who follows the teachings of Jesus. But in situations like these, an insecure person takes my place. It would be easy to cast a soft paintbrush to the whole picture and say that no harm comes from discreet gossip. But, in my heart, I know the truth. When we put down another person, the impact is felt, regardless of whether they hear it or not.

Why do I let my insecurities take me down this path? The real reason is that gossip takes the spotlight off of my life. By talking about someone else, it makes my troubles seem less enormous.

I hope that as I mature as a Christian, I will find the strength to exclude myself from gossip. The best course of action would be to remove myself from these gatherings where I know that mean-spirited talk will be the highlight. Jesus set the standard for unconditional love. By walking with Him on a daily basis, I know that someday I will find the power to withhold my judgment from others.

— Karen Talcott —

My Prayer

Forgive me, God, for the ways that I talk about others. Help me to recognize the signs when I am not acting in a Christian manner. Then guide me to be the best person you created me to be.

Amen.

79

God Sent Me an E-mail

Be devoted to one another in love.
Honor one another above yourselves.
~Romans 12:10

J im and I were devoted to and honored one another through most of our marriage. We got teased unmercifully by some family members, but most of the teasers have gotten divorced. Eventually, though, I got tired of being teased, put my needs before Jim's, and considered it a fair exchange.

Jim and I retired within six months of each other and settled into a new way of life. One morning, I sat absentmindedly deleting e-mails and wondered where our closeness had gone. My heart was overwhelmed with grief. Did anyone understand my agony?

God knew, understood, and sent me an e-mail. I clicked an e-mail containing a devotional, and within the e-mail was an invitation to join a "14-Day Romancing Your Husband Challenge." I was up for His challenge.

Just before Valentine's Day, the first e-mail challenge arrived, containing these four challenges:

Put a chocolate kiss in his briefcase, lunch bag or on the dashboard of his car, with a note that says, "I love you!" (I thought, "He does love his candy. I will put Junior Mints on the table near where he sits to watch TV.")

Write "I love you" on his bathroom mirror with soap or lipstick. (No lipstick, but doable. I will improvise.)

Send a romantic card to his workplace via snail mail. (He's not employed anymore, but I'll put a note by the coffeepot. He usually makes the coffee.)

Draw a candlelight bath and invite him to join you. (Never happened before, and after forty-five years, arthritis, and many more pounds, not happening now. I can light candles in the living room and snuggle close. A cushion usually separates us as I work on my computer.)

God's challenges made me consider other things I had stopped. I didn't surprise Jim with little gifts and cards, put notes in his lunch, bring him coffee in the evening, or make his favorite desserts. I stopped things that nurtured our loving relationship. I waited and waited for Jim to change. What a selfish and lonely way to live.

I've made small changes already, and Jim is responding. I don't ask him for help, but he joins me. Our closeness is returning, and our hearts are healing. My heart and e-mails remain open to God's invitations, as He encourages me.

God reached out to me when my heart was laid open from hurting. I'd still be waiting if He hadn't opened a door through His inviting challenge. A gentle flutter freed my spirit to God's gentle discipline and touched my broken heart.

— Marge Gower —

My Prayer

Dear Lord, help me find a way to alter my attention from what is missing in my life to the rich bounty that is lurking below the surface.
May I remember to surrender always to your healing grace. How blessed we are that you work in such mysterious ways.

Amen.

80

My Fading Looks

Charm is deceptive, and beauty is fleeting; but a woman who fears the Lord is to be praised.
~Proverbs 31:30

Many years ago, my father was walking down a city street on his way to pick up my mother at her office. He saw a woman ahead of him who was speaking vivaciously to another person. He was fascinated by how alive and vibrant she looked, and he stopped and said to himself, "What a strikingly beautiful woman."

After a moment, he continued on his way, but as he got closer to this woman on the street, he made a surprising discovery. The woman he had been captivated by was his wife—my mother—more lovely than ever to him after more than twenty years of marriage.

The older I get, the more I fret about my own ability to elicit that "Wow!" look from my husband that my mom still gets from my dad. Glancing through old photo albums can be a sobering experience. The beautiful hair I see in those old pictures is now flecked with gray (at least until I make it to my hair colorist), and wrinkles are taking over my once-smooth skin. Looking at the beautiful air-brushed and surgically enhanced movie stars in magazines makes a further dent in my self-esteem. I am no longer the young woman that my husband married.

But, deep down inside, I know that our relationship is based on more than an admiration of each other's looks. We're raising four wonderful children; we've built a home together; we share our faith in God; and, we have a history together that nobody else has experienced.

When my husband looks at me now, his eyes of love don't see the new wrinkles or gray hairs. They still see the same girl he married many years ago. In God's eyes, we are always beautiful. Thankfully, God has bestowed this same unconditional capacity to love—and a pair of rose-colored glasses—on our loved ones.

—Susan M. Heim—

My Prayer

God, thank you for making us "perfect" in your likeness. May we always see the same beauty in each other that your loving eyes see in us.
Amen.

81

The Comparison Trap

We do not dare to classify or compare ourselves...
~2 Corinthians 10:12

"Why can't my husband be more like her husband?" I silently wondered about a woman I knew at church. My spiritual life seemed to be growing in leaps and bounds, and yet I couldn't get my husband to do more than attend church on Sunday.

I longed to attend a Sunday school class together, but instead I attended a daytime Bible study alone, along with Mothers of Preschoolers (MOPS) and Wednesday night church dinners.

In comparison, that woman's husband seemed to be everywhere. He attended Sunday school and Wednesday night dinners with her, and sang on the praise team. He was with her and their kids at every family activity our church sponsored.

But an interesting thing happened. As I attended more events and got to be friends with her, she asked if she could share a concern with me. "My husband has anger issues, and we really need prayer," she said. I agreed to pray for her, but I was stunned. Her husband had anger issues? And I had wished my husband could be more like him…

Suddenly, I noticed all the positive things about my husband. Yes, he "only" attended church with me, but he attended every Sunday, faithfully and without complaint. He was a kind and loving husband and father, and an excellent provider for our family. I still wished his spiritual growth would more closely mirror mine, but I no longer played the comparison game with other husbands. Instead, I focused on my husband's positive attributes and prayed for his spiritual growth.

Years passed, and eventually we changed churches. The second Sunday we attended our new church, my husband said, "I guess we should find a Sunday school class." Shocked, I just nodded and followed him down the hall. Soon, he was attending Wednesday night suppers and family events with me. I was thrilled.

This experience has taught me several lessons. First, the comparison trap is a dangerous one. Because we only see the outward appearance, we don't know what happens behind closed doors in others' homes. Not only that, but comparisons lead to bitterness and envy. In choosing to look at my husband's positive attributes, I was no longer bitter, but content.

Second, prayer works! I prayed for my husband's spiritual growth, instead of just wishing for it. But don't think it happened overnight. It was literally years before I began to see small changes, and it's been nearly ten years since we first attended our old church. But, make no mistake, God did answer my prayers on His own timetable.

I am so thankful to God for not only growing my husband, but continuing to grow me as well. Currently, my husband is working toward his master's degree in theology. I am so proud of him. When I look at my husband now, compared to the man he used to be, there is no comparison. We have both been made new by God.

— Kelly Combs Keith —

My Prayer

Lord, help me to avoid comparisons to others. Erase envy from my thoughts and enable me to focus on the positive and abundant blessings in my life.
Amen.

82

Driving Lesson

Finally, brothers and sisters, whatever is true, whatever is noble, whatever is right, whatever is pure, whatever is lovely, whatever is admirable— if anything is excellent or praiseworthy—think about such things.
~Philippians 4:8

While driving to worship practice one morning, I was noticing the gorgeous flowers when, oops, I drove off the road. I drove along a bit more and noticed the neighbors had added new trim to their house. Uh-oh, off the road again. "Hey, look, they changed their…" Yup, you guessed it, off the road again.

By the time I got to church, I was more than a little bewildered. I don't normally drive that poorly, so I prayed in frustration, "Lord what's going on?" That's when I heard that still, small voice in my heart say, "You'll drive toward what you focus on!"

You see, my husband had been working a lot lately. He was a truck driver who had recently switched to over-the-road driving, which meant we only saw him on weekends. When he finally did get home, all I could think about was how he hadn't been there to help with the kids or fix the washer or complete the never-ending "honey-do list." I realized I spent so much time when he was home complaining to him about not being home that I wasn't enjoying the fact he was actually there! My complaining only led to arguments, hurt feelings, and a sense of relief when he left again, only to be followed by sadness and frustration.

Right then and there, I decided to change things. Instead of driving toward the frustration of him not being home, I decided to drive toward enjoying the fact that he was home. I tried to welcome my husband home as a happy-to-see-him wife, rather than the crabby why-aren't-you-home-more version. I saved the never-ending to-do lists until I could approach him kindly, asking for help rather than telling him what I needed done. As I changed my focus, I enjoyed our time together more, and our home became a much happier place.

As time has passed, the lesson I learned that day has become invaluable. I have found that the more I focus on the positive about my husband and our marriage, the more happy I am with him, and the more content I am with our marriage. When I drive toward negative things, soon it's all I see, and it becomes easy to get angry, frustrated and bitter. This doesn't mean that I just ignore the negative, but when I focus on all that is good and kind and wonderful about my husband, it puts the negative in proper perspective, and helps me to lovingly encourage a change for the better.

— Betsy Burnett —

My Prayer

Dear Lord, I know I will drive toward what I focus on. Help me to steer my thoughts toward the good things in my life and appreciate the admirable qualities of those around me.
Amen.

83

A Lesson in the Coffee Aisle

"But the things that come out of a person's mouth come from the heart..."
~Matthew 15:18

The old man in the coffee aisle dawdled along, his head drooping slightly as he eyed the vast array of choices in front of him. He grimaced at the sound of his wife's voice. "Will you hurry up? You'd think by now you'd know what kind of coffee we get." He reached out and pulled a green package off the shelf, then shuffled over and handed the bag to his wife. She took one glance, and her mocking tone was like a slap. "Stupid, this is regular grind. We use fine grind. Go back and get the blue one."

I wanted to reach out and hug the old man. I wanted to say to his wife, "How could you be so cruel?" But, of course, I didn't. I just thought to myself how glad I was that I wasn't a nag like that.

My shopping done, I headed home. Loading up the bags of groceries in my arms, I staggered to the door and kicked it open. I heaved a huge sigh as I let them drop to the floor. My husband, stretched out on the recliner watching TV, sat up. "Oh, I should have come out to help you."

"Yes, that would have been nice," I responded and turned to put away the groceries. Nursing resentment, I made sure the cupboard doors banged as I opened and closed them. The "ouch" I muttered when I bumped into a misplaced chair was louder than need be. And as I started cooking supper, I groaned audibly every time I had to move jars to get at something in the over-crowded fridge.

There wasn't much conversation as we ate on TV tables. As usual, I wished we could eat at a regular table like regular people do. As I prepared to wash the dishes, Don grabbed a dishtowel and started to tease me. I don't remember what I said, and nor does he, but whatever it was, it went into his spirit like a dagger. The look on his face was like that of the old man in the coffee aisle.

"Is that what you really think?" he choked out.

"Oh, I didn't mean it. I was just joking," I quipped back.

He looked at me, and his words stung because I knew they were true. "You wouldn't say it if it wasn't in your heart."

That night, I saw a bit of the old man's wife in me, and I prayed for God to show me how to love my husband. These days, I try to bite my tongue when criticism sits on the tip of it and to speak words of encouragement more often. Because of a chance encounter in the coffee aisle and my husband's courage to speak the truth to me, God has started to change me. In the process, my husband is enjoying the freedom to become the kind of man God meant him to be.

— Linda Mehus-Barber —

My Prayer

Lord, open my eyes to see the truth in my ways,
and may I have the willingness to change as you
direct. May I speak words of encouragement to
build others up and give them the confidence to
become all that you intend them to be.
Amen.

84

Bougainvilleas on the Bus Route

And my God will meet all your needs according
to the riches of his glory in Christ Jesus.
~Philippians 4:19

"We can't leave Montana!" I told God. "My children need to stay where they have family and teammates and school friends." I frantically prayed that God would work out the details for us to stay, but He didn't. Despite business counseling, strategic plans, and our best efforts, our school supply store failed. And like a black hole, it seemed to suck away my life.

After a difficult search, my husband found work in Arizona. With aching hearts, we packed up our four children and everything we owned and moved. It was the worst time to move my daughter. She was beginning her senior year in high school and would have to leave all her friends behind and start at a new school. She sobbed into my shoulder, and I comforted her as best I could, but I didn't understand the "why" either.

Since I wanted to stay strong for my husband and kids, I thought it was better for me to journal than to voice my grievances. I began to compile a list of things we had lost. I wrote several pages and thought of more things to add every day:

We lost our beautiful home and moved into an apartment.

We moved away from the kids' beloved grandmother.

We gave up one car only to have the other one break down in the move.

The kids have no friends here.

As the list grew longer, I also committed to reading my Bible every day, but I could not find peace. I kept getting stuck on Philippians 4:8, which admonished me to think about things that are praiseworthy. In my pain, I argued with God. "If I could think of anything that was praiseworthy, I would think about that!"

One morning on my way to work, I was staring out the window of the city bus when I noticed a bush covered in flowers that were bright fuchsia. I asked a fellow commuter for the name of that bush, for I had never seen flowers that color before.

"Bougainvillea," she replied.

"Okay, God," I silently prayed, "I will thank you for the bougainvilleas."

From that moment, I began to see those bright pink flowers everywhere! I remembered my promise and thanked God each time I saw them. When I returned home to my apartment, there were bougainvillea petals strewn by the wind all across my path. It melted my heart to feel Him reaching out and saying, "Trust me."

We have been in Arizona for several years, and now I journal my blessings, not losses. My daughter and oldest son met their wonderful spouses here. My two younger sons have seen opportunities open to them that were never available in Montana. And every year, God brings those bougainvilleas to bloom, reminding me of how His constant love changed my heart, even when I couldn't see Him.

— Lindy Schneider —

My Prayer

Lord, I give you all those things that make me anxious. I trust that you will work out all the details of my family's needs, including our financial needs. I pray that you will help me to focus on your blessings—those things that are praiseworthy—so that I might experience your peace in the midst of my trials.
Amen.

85

A Spirit of Thanksgiving

When I signed up to be Ray's helpmate "till death do us part," I never realized the depth of this commitment. My role became not only that of a wife, but as caregiver for more than twenty years.

Our journey together began July 17, 1982. Like any newly married couple, we had many dreams and aspirations. We had been married only four years when Ray was diagnosed with a rare form of degeneration of the cerebellum. In plain English, every motor area would be affected, and complete disability was inevitable.

By 1995, Ray was dependent upon me for almost everything. He needed my assistance for dressing, personal hygiene, and feeding. Caring for two young children, working as a part-time teacher, and caring for Ray filled almost every waking moment.

Although Ray's body was being ravaged by disability, his spirit continued to soar. His love and faith in God never waned. He had a real zest for life and always seemed to be thankful.

Ray and I both knew we still had plenty to be thankful for. By the grace of God, his mind stayed alert. He stayed engaged in life even though he lost most of his ability to communicate orally and experienced some hearing loss.

Despite all of his disabilities, Ray remained a positive teacher. He taught me so much about faith and trust—simply learning to take God at His Word.

I learned many lessons on this journey, but a primary one was the importance of cultivating a thankful spirit. No matter how negative our circumstances looked, we knew there was always something to be thankful for.

Many days were very hard and the struggles intense, but Ray was still with me, and he was a wonderful companion. His positive attitude was such a strength and encouragement to me. Ray possessed an uncanny sense of humor, which helped in keeping the stress level down.

I am eternally grateful that Ray was in my life for twenty-six years. His love, joy, and encouragement are still very much a part of my life today.

If you look closely, you will see there is always something to be thankful for. I believe the more you can cultivate a spirit of thanksgiving, the more your eyes are open to the beauty and the gifts in your life. So far, my life's journey has seen its share of hardship and pain. But through all of the difficulties, I believe that I have become stronger. I continue to see the beauty, love and faithfulness of God shine through, and I am thankful.

— Sandy Knudsen —

My Prayer

Heavenly Father, when the circumstances of life are getting me down, may you remind me that I have so much to be thankful for. Life can be hard, but I can still choose to be thankful. Open my eyes, Lord, so I can see the beauty around me.

Amen.

86

Being Thankful

... give thanks in all circumstances; for this is God's will for you in Christ Jesus.
~1 Thessalonians 5:18

"I'm sorry, but we've decided to give the position to another candidate." Those too-familiar words echoed through my mind as I set down the phone.

Another door closed. It had been more than a year since my company merged and I was laid off. At first, I was confident that twenty-five years of experience with the same employer would land me another job easily. However, the months dragged on, and the severance pay and the unemployment compensation ran out, forcing me to withdraw from my 401(k) to pay bills. I applied for every position available in my field. Still, no job offer. Every glimmer of hope dissolved into tears of disappointment. Daily, I appealed to God, asking for guidance and searching the Bible for answers. I desperately tried to hold onto hope and trust God to take care of me, but the future looked bleak. My prayers seemed to be unheard. At the age of fifty, I was no longer a desirable candidate, since a younger person could be trained for half my former income. I felt as if God had written me off like everyone else, and I was no longer necessary to society, other than my creditors.

A friend asked me if I would consider moving because, as an

empty-nester, I didn't need a big house. I was willing to make sacrifices, but giving up my house was not one of them. My home was my last bastion of security, an answer to prayer ten years before. I couldn't believe God would want me to move. This was the home where I would live in my old age, where my future grandchildren would visit.

One day, I came across the Bible verse, "… give thanks in all circumstances; for this is God's will for you in Christ Jesus" (1 Thessalonians 5:18). How could I do that? How could I be thankful for losing my job, running out of money, and possibly losing even more? To say I was thankful for these things would be hypocritical.

Then it occurred to me to thank God for what I had been given. I could thank God for my former career—the experience I had gained, the people I'd met and places I'd been. I thanked God for the home He had given me to raise my children and for the memories we had shared there. Then I realized God had given me the home when I needed it, and it had served its purpose. I had trusted Him with my past; therefore, I could trust Him with my future.

Being thankful allowed me to let go and opened my mind to other possibilities, even if it meant moving. Once I decided I was willing to move, I had three different job offers in other states. It's been more than six years since I moved. I love my new home, and God has blessed me beyond my expectations. I now know how to be thankful "in all circumstances."

— Marilyn Turk —

My Prayer

Dear Lord, thank you for everything you've given me. Knowing I have you to lean on when I am feeling worried makes my decisions easier. Remind me to place my trust in you, and in everything give thanks.
Amen.

87

In Everything Give Thanks

Thanks be to God for his indescribable gift!
~2 Corinthians 9:15

I woke early Thanksgiving morning and turned to greet my husband, only to encounter an empty pillow. Strange. I knew he had come in late from his evening shift. I couldn't imagine why he would be up early. With a shrug, I dismissed the thought and focused on getting up to face the busy day.

Yawning, I flicked back the covers and stumbled to my feet. Mornings were difficult as my mother's illness progressed. Hospice care proved to be a tremendous help, with an aide visiting on weekdays. But my husband and I handled the rest of Mom's care. My mother, a precious, godly woman, loved the Lord and had brought us to the truth of the gospel. At this time of her life, I yearned to ease her discomfort, but exhaustion threatened to overtake me from the increasing responsibilities.

Memories from the previous night haunted me. Not one of my mother's better days, it had been a struggle to prepare her for bed. She tried to hide the grimace of pain that stole across her features. I went to bed and cried myself to sleep. Overwhelmed, overtired, and over the edge, I fell asleep, praying for strength to care for her and for grace to let her go.

With these thoughts rolling through my mind, I went to check on the current situation. Hopefully, her night had passed without incident. Half asleep, I fumbled my way downstairs. I heard voices in the kitchen, and when I walked in, I found my missing spouse.

Clad in his red worn-out terrycloth robe, his feet encased in hunting boots, and a faint growth of beard shadowing his face, he stood by the kitchen counter. He flashed me a grin while offering Mom a cup of coffee. I blinked the sleep from my eyes.

"What are you doing?" I asked.

Mom gazed at my husband with maternal-in-law pride as he gently steered me back toward the stairs.

"Let me be with your mom this morning. Go rest a bit longer," he said. A soft smile filtered through my weariness. I viewed his unique attire with a raised eyebrow. He grinned. "I had to let the dog out quick, and it was snowing." With a giggle, I kissed his scruffy cheek and headed back to the welcome comfort of my bed.

The kindness of my husband helped me realize how much I had to be thankful for, even in the midst of my troubles. My mother went home to be with the Lord a week after Thanksgiving. We had our final holiday meal together, and my only sister came home from out of town to surprise her. We were all with my mother when she gave her last breath.

Years later, I still remember finding my husband tending to Mom's needs even though he was as tired as I was at the time. I'm thankful for my husband, for God's faithfulness, and for His enduring strength. Truly, in everything we give God thanks.

— Cynthia A. Lovely —

My Prayer

*Father God, although I don't always recognize your
gifts, remind me of your goodness each and every
day. Open my eyes to all I have to be thankful for,
no matter what situation I find myself in. And
let my lips call forth a continual thanksgiving,
fulfilling the will of God.*
Amen.

88

Laundry Days

Rejoice in the Lord always. I will say it again: Rejoice!
~Philippians 4:4

With seven kids, I do at least two loads of laundry every night, sometimes more depending on how dirty my husband got at work and how dirty the boys got at play. The dark load goes in after all of the kids have bathed and showered so that by the time there's enough hot water, that load is finished and ready for the dryer. My husband and I then jump in the shower, and when we're done, there's just enough hot water left to wash the light load. Typically by then, the dark load is dry and needs folding. The light load will get put in the dryer before we fall asleep or early in the morning as we all rise and start our day. Two loads a day equal fourteen loads a week. That's a lot of laundry!

When I've had a particularly exhausting day, the last thing I want to do is laundry. As I sort through the dirty clothes, I wonder why the boys can't seem to pull their socks apart instead of leaving them in balls, why the girls can't pull their underwear out of their shorts or pants, and why they all can't seem to sort darks from lights. "Why me?" I ask myself. "I didn't sign up for non-stop sorting, washing, drying, and folding!"

This is the time when I'm gently reminded that I did sign up for this. I did pray for this, and He answered. I did want more children, I did want a husband, and the laundry is just a small part of the bigger picture. God reminds me that my own laundry basket is overflowing with self-pity and bitterness when it needs to be overflowing with gratitude that the kids have clothes to wear and don't have a need for anything. We've been abundantly blessed in so many ways that fourteen loads is a small "price" to pay for what we've been given. As the clothes goes through the heavy cycle, so does my attitude. All the stresses of the workday—running children around, dinner on the go, housework, church activities, etc.—get wrung out of me as well.

At the end of each day, I take care of the laundry—and God takes care of me. It might be just allowing me to shed tears for no reason or a gentle reminder that I'm missing out on His purpose for me by focusing on something so inconsequential as laundry. He's definitely cleansed my heart more than fourteen times a week.

—Ami Tripp—

My Prayer

Father, help me to enjoy all parts of my life,
even those that seem challenging or monotonous.
Continue to wash away my frustrations and renew
in me a cleansed heart and soul. It is only through
You that we are truly clean.
Amen.

89

Serving Love

"Have you seen the one my heart loves?" Scarcely had I passed them when I found the one my heart loves. I held him and would not let him go...
~Song of Songs 3:3-4

Our lives had changed forever. My thirty-two-year-old husband, Erik, had tongue cancer. Within days of the diagnosis, he had gone through surgery to remove a portion of his tongue, had a tube placed for feeding, and began radiation and chemotherapy.

I couldn't bear to see him in so much pain. Because Erik couldn't speak, he mouthed directions to me, and I became his voice and his advocate, rarely leaving his side throughout most of his hospital stay.

The overworked nursing staff, with six to ten patients per shift, had little time for anything more than taking care of patients' essential needs. They rushed in and out of his room, making promises of bed changes, extra hospital supplies and even a bath, that under the circumstances, were unable to be fulfilled. So, as eleven days passed without Erik receiving a bath, anger rose in my heart, and I decided I would give him a sponge bath. Little did I know that this experience would be the most intimate moment he or I would ever share.

Placing a Please Do Not Disturb sign on the door, I assembled the preparations for his bath. Then I began by gently wiping his face, washing his eyes and downward to his neck, where sixty-four staples created a line from his ear, down his jaw line, and across his neck, ending directly under his chin. Gingerly, I washed around this very sore area, and silent tears ran down my cheeks. My heart was mourning the loss of his tongue and his face as I had always known it.

Maneuvering around tubes and drains and IV lines, I washed each inch of his body, thanking God for every bump, scar, mole and hair, cherishing every cell in Erik's body.

In my mind, I imagined Jesus washing the disciples' feet, lowering himself to a servant's role. I thought about how His gesture humbled the disciples.

In these moments, as I continued, I felt the deepest love for my husband I have ever known. To be his servant when he most desperately needed me humbled me completely. But then I realized how humbling it must have been for Erik to need help with his most basic needs.

My earlier anger with the nursing staff for their inattention melted into gratitude when I realized God had ordained this moment for Erik and me. Instead of feeling the embarrassment and humiliation of a stranger caring for him, Erik would feel my love as I, his helpmate, carried out the duties that honored him.

I looked up at Erik's face, blinking away my tears, and saw that he was crying, too. Without words, we were thinking the exact same thing, more connected than we had ever been. He looked into my eyes and mouthed, "I love you." After drying him off and covering him, I crawled into his hospital bed and laid my head on his chest, listening to my favorite sound: his heartbeat.

—Jennie Bradstreet Hall—

My Prayer

Dear God, how great is the example that Jesus showed His disciples. His love and service to His followers paved a way for all of us to find redemption. I pray that you would use me in service to others, that through the works of my hands, your light and love will shine through.
Amen.

90

That Was Love

...serve one another humbly in love.
~Galatians 5:13

I t was the basket. Not the Colombian roses or the diamond necklace or the theater tickets John bought me back when he sought
me as his wife. No, a cheap plastic basket of laundry taught me
what real love is. It was shortly after we wed, when I was dying.

Four months after we married, I entered the hospital. My body
had simply stopped absorbing any food or nutrition. Not one ounce.
I was literally wasting away. For weeks, my new husband stayed with
me in the hospital as doctors searched for the cause and performed
two surgeries to remove the portion of my system that Crohn's disease
had destroyed.

But something my husband did during my recovery spoke to me
of real love more than anything else. He did the laundry. Oh, not just
normal laundry. When recovering from this kind of surgery, well, let's
just say one's body doesn't always get timely signals for certain things.
And some of the laundry was, frankly, unpleasant. I was well enough
to handle the worst of it, and new bride enough to be embarrassed to
ask my husband to. One evening, I woke up from resting, desperate to
drop in a small load of no-longer-sexy underwear, when my husband
walked into the room with the laundry—freshly washed and folded.
I looked at him with tears in my eyes.

And I realized... that was love. Real, lasting love. Love that proves, through action, that it's willing to get down in the ugliest, most embarrassing parts of life with you. Love that accepts your most humiliating moments and carries you through them.

Through the tears, my eyes opened. I realized that sometimes love isn't expressed by flowers and jewelry, or even "I love you." The most powerful love is revealed through humble sacrifice. That's the love God wants us to show.

I decided I'd pay attention to the little things that spoke love, not just the big ones. You see, I saw that:

When John sent me out of state for three months so I could be with my dying father... that was love.

When he changed jobs so we could move closer to my mom... that was love.

When he took on a second job so I could pursue my dream of writing and editing... that was love.

When he fixes the computer I always break; when he insists our eggs be fixed the way I want more often than the way he prefers; when he calls me every day before he drives home... that all is love.

And it makes all the difference to recognize how my husband expresses love, rather than only noticing the flowers and candy. I've found a deeper, stronger romance. And God calls me to love sacrificially, as well. You see, I discovered that getting down in the dirty laundry together... well, that is love—love that makes marriages last.

— Diane Gardner —

My Prayer

Heavenly Father, please help me to recognize that love is revealed through humble sacrifices, not material things. May I pay attention to the little blessings in my life and show love to others through my actions.
Amen.

91

Trail to Tenderness

*Your eyes will see the king in his beauty and view
a land that stretches afar.*

~Isaiah 33:17

I t was raining when we reached the trailhead. Everything in me wanted to beg Corey to turn around and take me to a hotel. But I kept quiet, pulled a poncho over my head and got in step behind my husband on the Superior Hiking Trail. I struggled with my attitude all through the wet, muddy night, wondering why in the world I had ever agreed to such a trip.

"How are you holding up?" Corey asked, as we lay side-by-side in our sleeping bags.

I wanted to scream, "How am I holding up? Are you serious? I am miserable!" But instead I replied with a curt "surviving" as I rolled over to go to sleep.

I married a man who loves adventure, and for the first several years of our lives together, he was happy to go on his wilderness explorations without me. But when he requested I don a backpack and hike a portion of the Superior Trail with him, I knew I had to say yes even though I didn't want to. You see, a backpacking trip with my husband meant no running water and no toilets. It meant filtering drinking water from streams, fending off mosquitoes all day and sleeping in a tiny tent on the hard ground. Basically, it was the opposite of what I consider a relaxing getaway. But I love my husband, and I knew he wanted me to take part in his passion for the outdoors, so I agreed, albeit begrudgingly.

After a rainy first night, we awoke to sunshine, and God reminded me that love as He commands it is not just a warm fuzzy feeling, but a choice followed by action. So, on day two, I chose to love my husband by focusing on the good instead of the bad. That choice led to a gradual change in my attitude. I found that I enjoyed walking steps behind Corey through thick forests of trees without another soul around. I felt a sense of accomplishment when we reached the peak of Mount Trudee, and I was filled with awe when we stopped at an overlook with a view of the vast expanse of Lake Superior. When I finally quit feeling sorry for myself, I recognized what a gift it was to see Corey in all his rugged outdoor splendor. And I realized that eating a rice dinner out of a baggie on a tree stump beside my husband is actually pretty romantic.

Not only did I discover that I enjoy backpacking, but my decision to love Corey by taking part in his passion actually drew us closer together as a couple. I felt a deep tender connection to him by experiencing his enthusiasm for the outdoors, and he felt loved in a new way, knowing that I had stepped a million miles out of my comfort zone for his sake.

— Kim Harms —

My Prayer

Dear God, please help me to recognize opportunities to show love through my actions. Bless me with the foresight to look beyond my own desires and the courage to step out of my comfort zone.
Amen.

92

God Appears in Our Stillness

He says, "Be still, and know that I am God..."
~Psalm 46:10

P atience hasn't always been one of my virtues. I do most things quickly, and I expect others to do so, too. "Are you done yet?" "Are we there yet?" and "How long will it take?" are on my list of favorite things to say. Enjoying the journey has never been something I was good at. My eyes are always on the next thing to do, or the next place to go, or the next person to meet.

However, I married a man who has the patience of a saint. My husband is the type of person who can savor the moment. When we're vacationing at the ocean, I can look at the waves for a few minutes and then say, "Okay, let's do something else," while my husband can sit and enjoy the magnitude of the vast water for hours.

One day, while in Maine, we were sitting in our car, looking out at the ocean and watching the seagulls swoop up and down over the beach. One of them landed on the hood of our car and stared at me. We could see people in neighboring cars throwing bread to the other birds, but we didn't have any food. I couldn't understand why that seagull would have chosen to land on our car. And I certainly didn't know why he would look at me the way he did. He sat there for forty-five minutes, never taking his eyes off of me or moving a feather. I was so entertained by him.

Later that day, my husband told me that he had prayed something would keep me there, peacefully, in that car. He asked God to show me something that would make me slow down and just enjoy the day.

After years of marriage, I finally get him. I understand why he loves to linger on something for a long time. There is peace in each moment. There is God in that quietness. In those ordinary, simple pleasures, there is an extraordinary pay-off. I can hear my own thoughts, enjoy the presence of my husband in that stillness, and feel God's presence between us.

I've noticed that I don't experience God's best when I'm on the run. I don't feel His peace like I do when I'm just sitting with the man I gave my life to twenty-five years ago. I've learned to slow down, relish every moment, and be more like my husband, who taught me what God had in store all along.

— Marijo Herndon —

My Prayer

Lord, always make me grateful for the restful, quiet times in my daily life. Please help me to see you in the simple pleasures of each new day.
Amen.

93

On His Knees

> *In my distress I called to the LORD; I cried to my God for help. From his temple he heard my voice; my cry came before him, into his ears.*
>
> *~Psalm 18:6*

My dad probably never envisioned becoming a husband and father by the time he was nineteen. That was a lot of responsibility, but it was nothing compared to what was to come. Leap forward eleven years, and he and Mom had four daughters. With their combined incomes, my parents bought a big, new house. We moved in, but just a few months later, their marriage fell apart, and Mom moved out. That meant Dad not only had to raise four daughters alone, but he also had to pay for a two-income house with one income.

Becoming a suddenly single parent is always a struggle, but much more so for a man trying his best to raise girls. As in most families, Mom had done most of the nurturing. Dad knew little about cooking and less about housework. He hired babysitters and housekeepers, always with disastrous results. So, in the end, the five of us winged it. In the morning, I'd walk myself to school across the street. After school, I'd walk home and wait in the garage till my older sisters got home. I never told them that I was afraid to go into a house that had been empty all day.

Long after dark, Dad would arrive home. He was exhausted from ten-hour days, and though I didn't realize it then, he was also deeply troubled by the breakup with Mom. Even so, every night after work, he'd stop to spend time with us. We'd crawl all over him and tell him the complaints we'd waited to lodge against each other.

After a while, Dad would stand up and say, "Girls, I just need a few quiet minutes," and then he'd disappear into his bedroom.

Soon, we would start quarreling amongst ourselves, and we'd look around for our chief problem-solver.

"Dad!" we'd scream almost in unison. Then we'd burst into his room to tattle, and always find Dad kneeling by his bed in prayer. Those chaotic days are a blur now, but seeing Dad on his knees, humbling himself before God, is a sight I will never forget. His world had turned upside-down, draining his energy, but he knew where to go to renew his strength. He knew it was God who equipped him to get through another day as the suddenly single father of four. Whether he realized it then or not, he was also setting an example for his daughters.

These days, if I run out of strength, I remember where to go to renew the supply. There's a saying, "When times get tough, the tough get on their knees." Like my dad, I get on my knees, and I feel restored.

— Teresa Ambord —

My Prayer

Heavenly Father, I know that when my heart breaks, I can come to you to put it back together again, in your way and in your time. Help draw me near to you so I may listen to your voice of assurance that you whisper into my heart.
Amen.

94

P.S. Pray

I waited patiently for the LORD; he
turned to me and heard my cry.
~Psalm 40:1

Dear Son,

We all miss you. My heart aches with the choices that led you down this awful road that ended in a detention facility. I would do anything to fix your life for you, but I know that only you and the Lord can do that. I pray that your time in there will help you understand that real happiness can only come from doing what is right. Please know that we love you and are praying for you.

Love, Mom

P.S. Pray.

My tears blurred the words on the page before me. In all honesty, I didn't know what to say, didn't know how to fix things. The mother in me just wanted to make it all better, but I knew this was something I couldn't fix. My sixteen-year-old son would have to do this on his own, with God's forgiveness and help.

Exhaustion became normal as deep-rooted anxiety kept me agonizing and praying for my child. He was so lost. With big blue-green eyes filled with mischief and humor, my thoughtful, kind little boy grew to be a teenager I never dreamed he would be. His choices brought him to a darker and darker way of living. I watched as he changed before my eyes, becoming unhappy and angry, and spiraling steadily downward. It was tearing our family apart and my heart to shreds. Now the only way I could reach him was through occasional visits and mail, which they allowed him to read, then took away.

Each day, I began a new letter, tucking it into a card with a funny joke or a spiritual message. I prayed hard to know what to say, to know what my Father would have me tell my son that would make a difference. With each letter, I felt inadequate in my words, but I always ended with the same postscript: "P.S. Pray."

I received one letter from my son while he was incarcerated.

Dear Mom,

I am so sorry for all the things I've done. I miss you all so much, and I can't wait to get out of here to start over. I love you so much. I'm reading my scriptures every day, and I think this has been good for me. I needed to be here. I can't wait to come home.

P.S. I'm praying.

When my son came home, he had a new light in his eyes. He seemed focused, happy, and appreciative. We welcomed him with open arms, and soon his life was back on track.

One day, we were talking about his time in detention. I asked him what it was like, and he said it was part hell and part heaven. I asked him how it could ever be like heaven, and he said that with nothing to do but read scripture and pray, it had brought him closer to God than at any other time in his life. He told me how my letters made him homesick, but he always looked for my little postscript, which was like his compass.

We take it day by day now. We end each day with prayer as a family. My son has so much potential to be a great man who walks with the Lord. He still makes mistakes, but one thing is constant throughout his life: He prays.

— Susan Farr-Fahncke —

My Prayer

Dear Father in heaven, please walk with my child and never let him forget he belongs to you. Guide and protect him in every moment of every day, and remind him that you cherish him and forgive him. He needs you.
Amen.

95

Exchanged Gifts

Rejoice with those who rejoice; mourn
with those who mourn.
~Romans 12:15

I walked into the surgery waiting room with my devotional booklet in hand, fully intending to read it. But as I sat down and looked at the pages, it was hard to concentrate on anything but my husband. Though his particular surgery wasn't life-threatening, it demanded my full attention. I shifted my position and tried once more to read, but found myself being drawn to the conversation of a group of people to my right.

"The doctor should be calling us soon. She's been in surgery for a long time."

"Yes, but he told us the tumor was big."

"Let's join hands and pray."

I listened as this small group of people openly asked God for healing and strength. I glanced around the room and noticed uncomfortable looks, shuffling feet, and stares. I marveled at the courage of these Christians to publicly proclaim their faith without a thought for what others might think. I wanted to get up and add my own hands to their circle of prayer, but I held back. As usual, I was worried about what people would think of me. Instead, I silently joined in their prayer.

I learned they were friends and relatives of a young woman undergoing brain surgery. She was also a wife and mother of a small baby.

I listened carefully as they spoke of Christ and His power in their lives. Optimistic words of encouragement were exchanged, and they strengthened one another with discussions of family and church life. One man, a schoolteacher, offered humorous stories of classroom antics. The laughter these stories brought prompted me to ask myself if I could be so relaxed in a similar situation. They simply left everything in God's hands.

Finally, the call they'd been waiting for came. I watched intently as the young husband of the woman in surgery walked purposefully to the phone. The waiting friends and relatives were all standing. Their faces showed no worry, and there was no nervous hand-wringing. There was only the calm, hopeful demeanor of those trusting in God's will, whatever that might be.

When the young man hung up the phone, he wasn't smiling. Looking at each of them, he quietly said, "They got most of it, but couldn't get it all."

The mother of the young woman fell back into her chair and began softly crying. I could no longer sit silently. I rose, my own tears now falling, and walked over to this dear woman. I put my arms around her and held her.

The thought that I might be intruding crossed my mind. But her need to share her pain was evident in the way she immediately buried her face in my shoulder. I knew my feelings of apprehension were unfounded. We sat there with the eyes of the entire room on us, crying together.

After a few minutes, she wiped her eyes and looked at me. With mild surprise in her voice, she said, "It's so unusual for a total stranger to come up to someone like this."

As we sat and talked, I was glad I had decided to share their suffering instead of sitting passively. Not only was I able to show them I cared, but through their strong example, I was encouraged to be more open in my own faith: we helped each other.

—Denise A. Dewald —

My Prayer

Dear Lord, you know the situations and pain that all your beloved children are going through. Help us to reach out in love to others in their time of need. Use us to comfort them and lighten their burdens.
Amen.

96

God's Financial Plan

Be joyful in hope, patient in affliction,
faithful in prayer.
~Romans 12:12

I t was one of those "Dear Lord, what are we going to do?" moments. My husband Kyle called me from work to tell me he had just lost half his salary. Under normal circumstances, it would have been difficult, but I would have simply taken on more of our bills.

But at the time Kyle's architecture firm announced these drastic cuts, I was eight months pregnant and on bed rest, and I had already had to severely curtail my freelance writing business. Kyle and I had also been planning to have me become the primary caregiver of our son once he was born. This announcement sent us into a tailspin.

Later that night, when Kyle got home, we sat down with a stack of our monthly bills. But before we even began looking through them, we reached across the table to hold hands and pray. I don't remember exactly what we said, but I know that we praised God for His infinite goodness, for the plans He had for us, and for the plans He had for our little son, still inside my womb. We affirmed that though the news looked awful, we were not the one who was all-powerful, all seeing, and eternal. Our perspective was limited, whereas God's is limitless.

Then we took out a pad and a pencil, breaking down our monthly expenses to the penny, and we started slashing. No more lunches out. No more gourmet groceries. No more movie rentals. Instead, Kyle packed a lunch for work, we began shopping at a discount grocery store, and we checked out movies from the library.

We had always lived frugally, but now we had our expenses pared down to the absolute essentials. We took a deep breath, swallowed our pride and investigated public assistance. Unfortunately, we learned we made sixteen dollars too much per week to qualify.

We had no wiggle room, and we were scared. There were many nights when our fears and worries woke us up and prevented us from restful sleep.

That's when we stormed heaven. There's nothing quite like the power that comes from praising the Lord in the middle of your troubles. And anytime it seemed like our situation would stay bleak, we received unexpected assistance. A new—and easy—client hired me to write a monthly column. Our acupuncturist agreed to trade services. Our midwife cut her fees in half. These blessings helped us stay on track, and we thanked and praised God for each one of them.

It wasn't easy, and as we lived through it, it seemed like it would never end. But then, suddenly, seven months after our son was born, a new architecture firm contacted Kyle out of the blue. He was hired on the spot, and his new job more than replaced his lost salary and benefits.

Through this challenge, our marriage grew stronger, our faith increased, and we discovered our true priorities: God, then marriage and family. As long as we had our priorities straight, God would help us pay the bills.

—Jeanette Hurt—

My Prayer

Lord, we bring our current financial troubles to the foot of your cross, where you bore our burdens. Please, through the blessed help of your Holy Spirit, guide us with wisdom, discernment and understanding to see what your priorities are for our lives.

Amen.

97

Making the Big Decisions

*The seed will grow well, the vine will yield its fruit,
the ground will produce its crops, and the heavens
will drop their dew. I will give all these things as an
inheritance to the remnant of this people.*
~Zechariah 8:12

I had just dropped my twins off at pre-kindergarten and was standing in the school's parking lot talking with three other mothers of children in my kids' class.

"What public school are you zoned for?" we asked each other.

"Are you going to have your children tested for the gifted program?" another mother asked.

"We might try to get into the dual-language program," one of them said.

"We're looking at private schools," said another.

We went back and forth, comparing the pros and cons of the various schools and programs available for kindergarten.

This was a discussion I'd held with many other parents in the past year. After all, the transition to kindergarten is typically the time when parents have to make the "big decision" as to where their children will go to school. Will they attend a public or private school? A religious school or home school? How about a gifted program? Dual-language? Or a school for the arts?

As I stood in the parking lot that day pondering my choices—and feeling quite overwhelmed by all of the opinions being expressed by the other mothers—I felt pressured. Would my husband and I make the "right" choice for our children? Would they be missing out if we didn't follow the crowd or enroll them in an expensive school? The choice weighed heavily on my mind as I got into the car to go home.

Suddenly, I realized this wasn't a decision my husband and I had to make alone. As with any of the "big decisions" in life, we could ask God for guidance in finding the answer we sought. I felt a weight lift from my heart and did my best to put my worries aside. In the weeks and months ahead, my husband and I continued to seek advice from other parents, as well as our children's current teacher, but we also sought counsel from within, where God's steady presence dwells.

My boys are now thriving in kindergarten. Their teachers fit their personalities perfectly, and I really felt God's hand at work in guiding us in this decision. Ironically, we didn't choose the same school as any of the mothers who were in the parking lot with me that day. But we still keep in touch, and I know that they are happy with their choices, just as we are happy with ours. With a Christ-centered approach to decision-making, we figured out what was best for our family and our children's needs.

—Susan M. Heim—

My Prayer

Lord, please guide me in listening to your counsel when it comes to making the "big decisions" in my family's life. I know that you are totally accessible to us whenever we are in need. Help me to recognize your voice.

Amen.

98

Emergency Room Prayer

Answer me when I call to you, my righteous God. Give me relief from my distress; have mercy on me and hear my prayer.

~Psalm 4:1

fter rushing the kids to the bus stop, I found my husband immobilized by pain on our bathroom floor. He had suffered from occasional back pain, but nothing like the sudden and extreme pain of that morning. I sat next to him, tears silently streaming down my face, as we tried to figure out what to do. The only thing I could pray was, "Please, God, help him. Please help."

I finally called an ambulance, and we spent the remainder of the day in an emergency room hallway. He suffered back spasm after back spasm. My own body stiffened with each attack. The doctors pumped him full of painkillers and muscle relaxers, but nothing helped.

After six hours, and no sign of improvement, I went to the bathroom and cried in a stall.

"God, I don't even know what to ask the doctors to do. Please send help!"

Not long after my desperate bathroom-stall prayer, God sent help in the form of a neighbor's phone call.

"I saw the ambulance in your driveway this morning and wanted to check to see if you were all okay," she said.

"I'm afraid we're not okay. I'm at the hospital with my husband," I replied.

I filled her in on the details, knowing that she had suffered from serious back pain for years.

"You need to insist that he gets an MRI to find out what's going on. Keep insisting until they do one," she said.

I thanked her and immediately asked to see the attending doctor. The doctor wanted to keep the current course, but I insisted on an MRI.

The doctor warned me that it might take eight hours before there was an opening, and I prepared myself for a long night of waiting.

Not more than a half-hour later, the orderlies came to take my husband for the MRI. The doctors and nurses said they had never seen anyone get in that quickly. I smiled, knowing that God had paved the way for us as an answer to prayer.

The MRI showed two bulged disks. After an injection into the affected disks, my husband finally experienced relief. And praise God, after months of therapy, he received complete healing.

That day in the emergency room reminded me that no matter how simple the prayer—or where it is offered from—God is listening and ready to help us. We just need to humbly ask for help.

—Amelia Rhodes—

My Prayer

Lord, please help us to remember to pray humbly, no matter what the situation or wherever we might be. May we never be too busy to stop and ask for your ever-present help.
Amen.

99

God Was at the Wheel

I call on you, my God, for you will answer me; turn
your ear to me and hear my prayer.

~Psalm 17:6

A s my husband and I sat in church on the Sunday before Thanksgiving, we listened to the traditional message about giving thanks to God for our many blessings. This sermon was especially meaningful as I thought back over the past year.

In late March, my husband, daughter and I were driving home from a wedding through the mountains to our rural hometown. I fell asleep in the passenger seat, and my next memory was being in a rehabilitation center ten days later with a broken pelvis and ribs, collapsed lung and traumatic brain injury. My husband and daughter were treated and released for minor injuries.

I was confined to home and a wheelchair for two months. Without the support of our church family and community, I would have spent much longer in the rehabilitation center, but they took over sitting with me during the day while my husband was at work, providing meals and praying for our recovery.

Through the prayers and support of our family, friends and community, I am back at work part-time (much earlier than the doctors predicted). For me, the biggest challenge was having to rely on others to take care of daily tasks, such as grocery shopping and meal preparation.

This unexpected accident changed our lives, yet we all emerged stronger. My son learned to be responsible for getting his schoolwork done by himself. My daughter learned the value of a church family, and that she could keep going and finish her college semester far away from home. My husband and I remembered the value of family and friends during tough times. Through this experience, I've learned the power of prayer, and that even though God provides challenges, we become stronger in meeting them.

— Nancy Kershaw —

My Prayer

Father, thank you for my life and all the blessings you have given me. Even in times of crisis, you are there to help heal the situation. When our bodies are weak, you find miraculous ways to comfort us and give us the strength to go on.
Amen.

100

The Trees Needed to Be Cut

*Now faith is confidence in what we hope for and
assurance about what we do not see.*
~Hebrews 11:1

I t was hurricane season again in Florida and time for the palm
trees to be cut. We were always warned before hurricane season
to prepare and cut back the palm fronds and coconuts. They
could become missiles during a hurricane, doing great damage
to the windows in the house.

One morning as I left the house, I decided to ask God for help in
finding a tree cutter. I quickly said a short prayer asking God to send
someone to my house who could cut the trees back while offering to
perform the work for a reasonable cost. I then went about my day
without giving it a second thought. I knew that once my prayer had
been asked, I needed to have faith that God would help me out.

That night as I played in the front yard with my kids, a little red
pick-up truck entered the neighborhood. The driver drove around for
a while before coming back to stop directly in front of my house. He
stopped to make small talk and admire my collie.

For some reason, I asked if he cut trees and, sure enough, he did—and he had time to take care of them that night! Of course, the price was going to be a deciding factor in the whole deal, but the price he quoted was the exact number in my head.

I asked for his business card when he was done. It read: *Respectful Tree Service, Doing God's Work for 15 Years.* A jolt ran through my body as I read the words. I did not need any more proof that God had helped me that day.

— Karen Talcott —

My Prayer

God, thank you for allowing us to send short quick prayers up to you in Heaven. You always hear our needs, be they big or small, and then respond in your most loving way.
Amen.

101

Carried Home

Take my yoke upon you and learn from me,
for I am gentle and humble in heart,
and you will find rest for your souls.
~Matthew 11:29

I didn't say anything, nothing. I just stayed balled up in my sleeping bag, unable to force myself up. Just the thought of moving made me cringe.

"Rise and shine!" our guide, Beth, chirped into our tent for the third time.

Everyone around me groaned.

Today was the last day of our "Survival Course." If I made it through today, I would get full credit. But I was sick. So sick. My feet were sore, my back was sore, my whole, entire body was sore. I literally ached all over. Some of my pain was caused by the three weeks of hiking and camping out in the freezing elements. But most of my pain was simply because I was sick. Achingly, disastrously sick.

Finally, I dragged myself out of my sleeping bag, literally wobbling as I tried to stand. What was I going to do? I could barely walk, yet we would be hiking all day. All day! My bones ached. They felt brittle, like they would crumble into pieces at any minute. And it wasn't just the agonizing pain or the freezing cold—there was my backpack, too. It was heavy beyond belief. So heavy! It was backbreaking, even on the best of days. Today, I could barely lift it.

Still, painfully, I slouched into it, trembling from the weight.

What else could I do? There was certainly no turning back, as we had been hiking for over three weeks. There was no staying here, either, since the camp was already disassembled. We were out in the middle of nowhere. It was hopeless. Although I knew I was headed for tragedy, I started to hike.

My heart plummeted when the snow began to fall and kept falling. Finally, I had to stop. I couldn't go on, not another step. Through my tears, I started praying to my Heavenly Father. I asked Him to help me, to somehow get me through this and safely home.

Slowly, I started to walk again, still praying as I trudged along.

But soon—it was so strange—I noticed my backpack felt lighter. And then I couldn't even feel it! I really couldn't, not at all. I kept checking to see if it was even on my back. And then I noticed something else: I couldn't feel my body. All the terrible aches and pains were gone.

It was astounding. Truly.

My Heavenly Father had heard my prayers. No, I wasn't brought into a nice, warm, toasty cabin. But in my hour of need, He had lightened my load. My burdens had been lifted. My Father carried me home.

—Melanie Marks—

My Prayer

Heavenly Father, in our hour of need, you hear our cries of pain and come to lighten our load. Our burdens are lifted, and we are reminded that you are ever present in these trying moments.
Amen.

Meet Our Contributors

The bios that follow represent the most recent ones we have for the contributors who wrote the stories in this book. Some are current today, and some were current as of the first publication of their stories in our past devotionals books.

Debbie Acklin loves sharing moments of her life with you through her stories. From her perspective, life is a great adventure and should be lived with passion, faith, and a large dose of fun. Surrounding herself with family increases the joys and blessings of that life. E-mail her at d_acklin@hotmail.com.

Debbie Albeck is a retired Respiratory Therapist, residing in Southeast Florida with her husband Bob. Debbie enjoys spending time and doting on her children and granddaughter. She is an active volunteer in her church and community, and takes great pride in participating as a trained poll worker. E-mail her at Debbie.albeck@ gmail.com.

Teresa Ambord was an accountant for many years before becoming a full-time writer. Now she writes full-time from her home in far Northern California, surrounded by the posse of small dogs that decorate her life. Teresa makes a living writing for business, but her heart is in writing about her family, faith and pets.

Barbara Brady is a retired RN who lives with her husband Merris in Topeka, KS. Barbara enjoys reading and believes everyone has stories to tell.

Rhonda Brunea is a mom and writer living happily in her little miracle home in the country. She is kept company by her two youngest kids, a bunch of dogs, cats and birds, and two sheep who never fail to entertain.

Betsy Burnett is a freelance writer, crafting event planner and serves as a year-round volunteer with Operation Christmas Child. Betsy currently lives in Illinois with her husband, daughter and fur babies. In her free time, she enjoys riding her bike, reading, and crafts of all types. E-mail her at burnett.betsy@gmail.com.

Dianne E. Butts has over 250 publications in magazines and books, is the author of *Deliver Me: Hope, Help, & Healing through True Stories of Unplanned Pregnancy* (www.DeliverMeBook.com), and is an aspiring screenwriter. She enjoys riding her motorcycle with her husband Hal and gardening with her cat in Colorado. www.DianneEButts.com.

Leah Clancy has worked in youth, missions, and women's ministries for fifteen years. She is a native Texan, mother of four, and loves being a pastor's wife. Her interests include writing, scrapbooking, saving money, and living simply. Her other devotions for moms and contact information can be found at www.21piecesofbrave.blogspot.com.

Gayle Allen Cox is an award-winning freelance writer from Spring, TX. Her byline appeared in *Chicken Soup for the Soul: Twins and More*, and has appeared in *The Dallas Morning News*, the *Fort Worth Star-Telegram*, and in various other newspapers and magazines. E-mail her at gaylecox@charter.net.

Michelle Crystal is the wife of one and the mother of four. She has written three full-length novels that are being considered for publication, and is actively working on her fourth. Michelle enjoys exercise, working with children, and writing. E-mail her at michellecrystal@comcast.net.

A storyteller at heart, **Michele Cushatt** has written four books and speaks internationally on leadership, resilience, and faith in the hard places. A three-time cancer survivor, Michele is a (reluctant) expert on trauma, faith, and our deep need for authentic connection. She and her husband have six children, and live outside of Denver, CO. Learn more at www.MicheleCushatt.com.

Denise A. Dewald has been writing Christian material for over twenty-five years with numerous publications to her name. Denise enjoys reading, needlework, music, her family and pets. One of her poems has been made into a song and aired on Family Life Radio. E-mail her at 83.kmgs@gmail.com.

Sally Dixon is an Australian author and textile artist who runs a small business called Sally Dixon Creations. Her creative projects include writing stories, making crosswords, designing sewing patterns, and stitching miniature felt gifts. She has been published in various books and magazines and has authored an international craft book.

Neither blindness nor unthinkable tragedies have prevented **Janet Perez Eckles** from becoming an award-winning author, international speaker, Master Spanish interpreter and founder of JC Empowerment Ministries. She helps thousands overcome fear and see their life through the eyes of tenacity, faith and courage. Learn more at www.janetperezeckles.com.

Shawnelle Eliasen is mother to five sons and wife to Lonny. She home taught for twenty-five years and now enjoys convertible rides, picnics, and other adventures with Lonny and their Labrador Little Girl.

Susan Farr-Fahncke is the founder of 2TheHeart.com, where you can find more of her writing and sign up for an online writing workshop! She is also the founder of the volunteer group, Angels2TheHeart, the author of *Angel's Legacy*, and contributor to more than sixty books, including many in the *Chicken Soup for the Soul* series. Visit her at www.2TheHeart.com.

Elizabeth Fenn received her BS in nursing from Purdue University in 1994. She worked as a pediatric oncology nurse at the National Institutes of Health (NIH) for nine years. She and her husband continue to raise three children and enjoy watching their transition into adulthood. Elizabeth is active in her local church and serves in leadership in the Women's Ministry.

Peggy Purser Freeman, award-winning author, novelist, editor, journalist, and motivational speaker, writes books to remember, including *The Coldest Day in Texas* (TCU Press), *Spy Cam One*, *Cruisin Thru Life*, *Teach Writing without a Pencil*, *Swept Back to a Texas Future*. Follow her on Facebook, X, Pinterest, and Instagram. Learn more at PeggyPurserFreeman.com.

Meagan Greene Friberg is completing her BA degree after taking a thirty-year detour to raise her children. She cherishes time with her husband, their children, grandchildren, and two big, happy dogs. She enjoys writing short stories, camping, church activities, and long lunches with friends. E-mail her at mgreenefriberg@aol.com.

Diane Gardner holds a Bachelor of Arts and a Master of Arts degree in mass communication and journalism from California State University, Fresno. She is a full-time writer and editor. Diane lives in the San Francisco Bay Area, where she enjoys traveling, painting, reading, and attending local community events.

Jenny R. George lives on a five-acre hobby farm north of Coeur d'Alene, ID, with her husband and two children. When she's not writing, she's enjoying the glorious North Idaho outdoors hiking, biking, horseback riding, and taking in stunning mountain and lake views.

Marge Gower is a retired teacher's aide, who worked with special needs children. She lives in Auburn, NY with her husband Jim and their French bulldog, Bugg. Marge has a devotional published in the *Love Is a Verb* anthology and many newsletters. She writes children's stories and inspirational pieces.

Jennie Bradstreet Hall is a freelance writer. She is a wife and a mother to three amazing adult children and now a grandma to seven grand-babies. Her family has gone through many struggles and adventures including a premature baby, a house fire, three floods, cancer, the death of a child and grandchild, and traveling twenty-nine states, all of which have given Jennie a unique perspective on life. E-mail her at bejennie1@gmail.com.

Kim Harms is the author of *Life Reconstructed: Navigating the World of Mastectomies and Breast Reconstruction*, and is currently under contract for her second book. She is a two-time breast cancer survivor with a BA in English from Iowa State University. Learn more about her at kimharm.net or on Instagram @kimharmslifereconstructed.

Kathie Harrington holds a master's degree in speech pathology from Truman State University. She has a private practice, Good Speech, Inc., in Las Vegas, NV. Kathie is a seasoned author, and this is her second contribution to *Chicken Soup for the Soul*. Contact her at www.

kathiesworld.com or kathieh2@cox.net.

Christina (Stina) M. Harris received her BA in Literature from Ramapo College and is a member of the National English Honor Society. A freelance writer, she plans to have her first novel published sometime this year. Please feel free to contact her via e-mail at charris110384@gmail.com.

Carol Hartsoe and her husband, Joel, live in Bear Creek, NC. She is blessed that her family lives nearby and enjoys spending time with them. Her hobbies include scrapbooking and gardening. A retired teaching assistant, Carol now spends time writing for children. E-mail her at chartsoe@ec.rr.com.

Linda A. Haywood received both her Bachelor of Social Work and Master of Social Work degrees from Eastern Michigan University. She has worked with seniors, those receiving mental health services and survivors of domestic violence. Linda plans to writes inspirational books for adults. E-mail her at lhaywood45@yahoo.com.

Marijo Herndon is an artist and writer living in New York with her husband, Dave, and resident feline, Piper Pickles. She has written several stories for the *Chicken Soup for the Soul* series, NightsAndWeekends. com, *Not Your Mother's Book* series, *One Touch from the Maker*, *Simple Joy*, and *The Daily Gazette*.

Darlene Hierholzer is the mother of three children, unexpectedly losing her beloved son, David, in 2008. She worked with her daughter, Dana Hierholzer, the author of this piece, to share a story of a comforting soul during that heartbreaking time. Currently, she is helping her daughter with her first novel, *Something to Believe In*.

Ann Holbrook lives in Northwest Arkansas. She has been published in *The Storyteller*; *The Ozarks Mountaineer*; anthologies including: *Writing on Walls*, *Voices*, *Echoes of the Ozarks*, *Skipping Stones*, and *Chicken Soup for the Soul: Tough Times, Tough People*. She is working on an inspirational book for cancer patients and their families.

Mary Hughes loves writing true stories that encourage and inspire people to live more faith-filled lives. She has a devotional newsletter, "Christian Potpourri," now in its eighth year. E-mail her at christianpotpourri@hotmail.com or visit her website at christianpotpourri.com.

When not spending time with her husband and son, **Jeanette Hurt** writes books, articles and essays, primarily about food, wine and travel. She also teaches culinary and writing classes. Follow her on X @JHurtAuthor, or visit her website at jeanettehurt.com.

Robbie Iobst is a writer and speaker living in Waco, TX with her husband John, son Noah and Chihuahua/Pug Thor. Her stories have appeared in ten *Chicken Soup for the Soul* books, and she has written three books all available on Amazon. E-mail Robbie at robbieiobst@ hotmail.com. or learn more at www.robbieiobst.com.

Vicki L. Julian is a freelance editor, the author of eleven books, and a contributor to numerous magazines, newspapers and anthologies, including the *Chicken Soup for the Soul* series. She also serves as a Stephen Minister in her church. Learn more at https://www. vickijulian.com.

Deborah L. Kaufman has enjoyed working in international adoption, domestic foster care, and teaching English to middle- and high-school students. She is a wife, mother, and proud grandmother. Deborah enjoys reading to excess, teaching Bible study, and writing inspirationals and romantic suspense. You may e-mail her at dlkaufman@ bellsouth.net.

Kelly Combs Keith is thankful she learned the gift of resilience and contentment in her marriage before losing her husband of seventeen years to cancer. Happily remarried, she shares five children and three grandchildren with her husband.

Nancy Kershaw is retired from the Oregon State University Extension Service after thirty-eight years. Nancy and her hubby live in Netarts, OR, but also live part time in Conshohocken, PA where their daughter, son-in-law and grandchildren live. She enjoys traveling/ cruising, spending time with family, reading and walking.

Karen Kilby lives in Kingwood, TX, with husband David. She is a Certified Personality Trainer with CLASServices, Inc., as well as a speaker for Stonecroft Ministries. Karen enjoys sharing her life experiences and has had several stories published in *Chicken Soup for the Soul* books, as well as other publications. Contact her at krkilby@

kingwoodcable.net.

Doing soaking worship on her keyboard is a primary passion for **Sandy Knudsen**. She and her husband, Mike, are involved with various prayer groups. Mike was diagnosed with Parkinson's shortly after they were married but they still spend much time in prayer; praying for family and friends and for our nation and the world. Sandy also enjoys activities with family and friends. E-mail her at worshipatrest@gmail.com.

Laurie Kolp has a Bachelor of Science in Curriculum and Instruction from Texas A&M University. She taught school for twelve years and although she continues tutoring children with dyslexia, her true love is writing. Laurie lives in Southeast Texas with her husband, three children and two dogs. Contact her at www.conversationswithacardinal.blogspot.com.

K.P. lives and works as an educator on the west coast with her now ten-year-old child, her husband, and a motley assortment of pets. She enjoys writing, teaching, and all outdoor activities. Her current goal, to master Sudoku, is progressing slowly and painfully.

Madeleine Kuderick is passionate about writing stories and poems that touch the heart. Her work appears in *Chicken Soup for the Soul*, *A Cup of Comfort*, Hallmark Gift Books and similar anthologies. She speaks at conferences hosted by the International Reading Association and the Council for Learning Disabilities. Learn more at www.madeleinekuderick.com.

Dorothy LaMantia writes stories of everyday faith and redemption in her study overlooking Barnegat Bay, NJ. A former English teacher, she has won an award for reporting from the Catholic Press Association. This is her third contribution to the *Chicken Soup for the Soul* series. E-mail her at dotelama@aol.com.

Robyn Langdon has a bachelor's degree from Colorado State University and a continuing life degree from Jesus, who teaches her challenging, exciting things every day. She is a daughter of The King, a wife, a mother, a pastor's wife, and a writer—in that order. Visit her blog at www.robynatthecrossroads.blogspot.com.

Kathryn Lay is an author of many children's books as well as stories and articles for children and adults. She and her family live in Texas. Learn more at kathrynlay.com or e-mail her at rlay15@aol.com.

At age thirty-three, **Kim Leonard** was diagnosed with breast cancer. Even though it was one of the most difficult times in her life, it was also when she drew near to God. Cancer ignited a deep desire to share her faith with others. She created and leads a community of women called Behold and Become. Kim and her husband Brad have three girls. She enjoys spending time with family and friends.

Janeen Lewis is a writer and teacher. She lives in Kennesaw, GA with her husband Jesse and two teenagers, Andrew and Gracie. She has been published in more than a dozen *Chicken Soup for the Soul* anthologies and several magazines and newspapers across the country.

Cynthia A. Lovely, from New York, is a freelance writer with over sixty published articles and stories in various periodicals. She co-authored a book titled *Aging Fabulously:52 Devotions Sure to Give You a Faith-Lift* which was released this year and is available through Amazon. E-mail her at cllyrics@gmail.com or visit cynthiaalovely.com.

Melanie Marks has had over fifty stories in magazines such as *Highlights*, *Woman's World* and *Teen Magazine*. She's had four children's books published, and numerous teen novels including: *The Dating Deal*, *A Demon's Kiss*, *Paranormal Punch*, and *The Stranger Inside*. Learn more at byMelanieMarks.com or e-mail her at melanie@byMelanieMarks.com.

The marriage described in her story is the second marriage for **DV Mason**, thus the commitment to keep it happy. DV enjoys writing nonfiction short pieces. She divides her time between being a wife, grandmother, and skills trainer for their adult son who has disabilities, and caring for her ninety-five-year-old mother.

Before she even learned to write her name, **Ann McArthur** was dictating stories to her mother, who patiently typed them. She graduated from seminary and continues to tell stories in the women's Bible studies that she teaches. She is about to release her first novel, *Choking on a Camel*.

Linda Mehus-Barber is a retired teacher who lives in Kelowna, BC with her husband, an old cat, and an amazing Border Collie. Their little cabin overflows with the love and joy that comes from seeking life's simple pleasures.

Michelle Close Mills has been a frequent contributor to the *Chicken Soup for the Soul* series as well as many other anthologies. She and her family are longtime residents along the Florida Gulf Coast. Learn more about Michelle www.authorsden.com/michelleclosemills.

Adjunct reference librarian **Shelley Mosley** has co-written nine books and one novella. She also writes articles and reviews books for professional journals. One of her stories, "Man and Car: A Love Story," was in *Chicken Soup for the Soul: Family Matters*. E-mail her at deborahshelley@mindspring.com.

Kathryn Nielson received her BA in Communications with a writing emphasis from Moody Bible Institute. She lives in Peoria, IL, with her husband and two children. In her spare time, she loves spending time with her family, reading, drinking coffee, and snuggling with her cat.

Tammy Nischan is a Christian teacher, speaker, and writer who resides in Grayson, KY, with her husband, Tim. She is the mother to four children on earth and two in heaven. Tammy enjoys sharing her photography and devotional thoughts on her blog, "My Heart… His Words." Learn more at www.tammynischan.blogspot.com.

Andrea Arthur Owan is a writer, Bible teacher, health and fitness professional, and Ordained Senior Chaplain specializing in grief and forgiveness. She and her husband, Chris, are relishing lake and coastal life in the Pacific Northwest after twenty-five years in the Southern Arizona desert. Her current hobby is house remodeling. Connect with her at andreaarthurowan.com, or andreaarthurowan@gmail.com.

Charles Owens hails from Trinity, NC. He received his undergraduate degree in business from Point Loma Nazarene College in San Diego and his Master's degree from the Naval War College. Charles and his wife Sonja have three children and enjoy traveling and working in Christian ministry.

David Ozab is currently writing his first non-fiction book, *Her Name is Anna*, which tells the story of his daughter's cleft surgery and struggles with speech. This devotional is excerpted from his book. He also writes about his life as a stay-at-home dad at FatherhoodEtc.com.

Michelle Rayburn hosts the "Life Repurposed" podcast and is the author of ten books covering topics of relationships, parenting, humor, and Bible study. She's been married for over three decades, appreciates time with her two grown sons and their wives, and adores being a grandma to their littles. Learn more at www.michellerayburn.com.

Amelia Rhodes is the author of *Pray A to Z: A Practical Guide to Praying for Your Community*. She lives in Michigan with her husband and children where she also serves as the Director of Discipleship Resources for Ada Bible Church. When the Michigan weather cooperates, she enjoys hiking and kayaking with her family. E-mail her at amelia@ameliarhodes.com.

Shelley Ring lives near Pikes Peak, CO, with her family and two dogs. She is a "real mom" to her stepson and two biological children. When she isn't playing in the sunshine (and sometimes even when she is), Shelley writes professionally for marketing and publishing industries.

Clara Riveros was born in Colombia, South America. She has three daughters and lives with her youngest, Melissa, who has Down's syndrome. Clara retired and enjoys spending time with her six grandchildren, but she spends most of it with Melissa's busy training schedule for Special Olympics.

Theresa Sanders recently retired from running "Tenderly Theresa," a daily inspirational microblog with over 100,000 followers. A frequent contributor to the *Chicken Soup for the Soul* series and award-winning technical writer, she loves spending time with her husband of forty-eight years, four beloved children, and six adored grandchildren.

Lindy Schneider is an author, illustrator, and award-winning playwright. This is the twelfth *Chicken Soup for the Soul* book in which her stories have been published. She is currently writing a new musical with her husband and lyricist, Tom Schneider. *Letters, the Musical* is based on a heartwarming true story about a box of letters that is found sixty years after they were written and how those letters impact the lives of those they touch. E-mail her at Lindy_schn@yahoo.com or learn more at LettersTheMusical.com.

Loretta D. Schoen grew up in São Paolo, Brazil, and Rome, Italy, and now resides in Florida with her husband, two cats, and two dogs. She enjoys traveling, working with abused animals, and spending time with her grandson, Aiden. She is currently writing medical stories to inspire and empower patients.

Bev Schwind has published anthologies and devotions, and written five books. She was Patches on the television show, *Patches and Pockets*, for eighteen years. A retired nurse, Bev teaches weekly at a jail and rehab center. She and her husband of sixty years, Jim, have won tennis medals in Senior Olympics. E-mail her at Bevschwind@ hotmail.com.

Michelle Shocklee is the author of several historical novels, including *Count the Nights by Stars*, a *Christianity Today* fiction book award winner, and *Under the Tulip Tree*, a Christy and Selah Awards finalist. Married to her college sweetheart and the mother of two grown sons, she makes her home in Tennessee. Learn more at MichelleShocklee.com.

Jennifer Smith is a nursing student who is passionate about life and writing. She loves to spend time with her wonderful husband and her two sons. She hopes that her stories will point the readers to Christ and that He alone will be glorified.

Jennifer Stango received her BS in nursing from the Indiana University of Pennsylvania in 1992 and practiced as a critical care nurse until she became a stay-at-home mom with her four children. She enjoys running, volunteering at her church, and spending time with her family.

Diane Stark is a Jesus follower, a wife, a mom of five, and a freelance writer. She loves to write about the important things in life: her family and her faith. She is a frequent contributor to the *Chicken Soup for the Soul* series and a contributing editor at *Guideposts* magazine. She can be reached at DianeStark19@yahoo.com.

Amy L. Stout is a wife, mommy, and autism advocate who loves travel, coffeehouses, books and, most importantly, Jesus! As a child of the King, her tiara is often missing, dusty, bent out of shape or crooked, but she will always and forever be his treasured princess.

Sandra Diane Stout received her Associate's degree in Business Studies from Indiana University Kokomo and is a graduate of the

Institute of Children's Literature. She is a retired secretary at Indiana University Kokomo and is an accomplished pianist. She writes children's nonfiction. E-mail her at dstout@iu.edu.

Terrie Todd is the author of ten historical and split-time novels, a newspaper columnist, playwright, blogger, and winner of several Word Awards and the Braun Book Award. Terrie lives with her husband, Jon, in Portage la Prairie, Manitoba. They have three grown children and five grandsons. Find her at www.terrietodd.blogspot.com.

Ami Tripp works full-time for the University of California, Davis, and is a wife and busy mother of seven (three are hers and four are his). She is also working on her Master's in Education. In her spare time, she enjoys reading, writing, shopping, and cuddling with her children. Find more of her writings at www.blendingfamilies1.blogspot.com.

Author **Marilyn Turk** has written over twenty historical and contemporary novels and novellas, plus a devotional book, *Lighthouse Devotions*. Marilyn also writes devotions for *Walking in Grace*, and other *Guideposts* publications. She and her husband Chuck enjoy visiting lighthouses, playing tennis, fishing and boating. At her church, Marilyn sings in the choir and leads a women's group.

Audrey Valeriani is an author, columnist, self-esteem and relationship coach, board chair of Self Esteem Boston, and founder of The R.E.A.L. Women's Club. Her book, *Boot Camp for the Broken-Hearted: How to Survive (and Be Happy) in the Jungle of Love*, was a finalist in the National Best Book Awards 2008. Visit her website at www. bootcampforthebrokenhearted.com; e-mail her at theaccidentalexpert@ comcast.net.

Mary Z. Whitney lives in Leavittsburg, OH with her husband John and their dog, Max. They enjoy gardening, traveling and spending time with their grandkids. Mary contributes to *Angels on Earth* magazines, and is the author of two books, *Max's Morning Watch* and *Life's A Symphony*.

Pam Williams is a freelance writer, retired pastor's wife, mother, and grandmother. Her articles and stories have been published in various cat and Christian magazines, as well as several *Chicken Soup for the Soul* books. She is the author of *A to Z Devotions for Writers*.

Angela Wolthuis lives in the woods of Alberta with her husband and three boys. She finds inspiration for her writing in everything around her, and loves to quilt, craft and be active. Last year she published her first book. E-mail Angela at angwolthuis@me.com.

Meet Our Authors

Susan M. Heim is a longstanding editor and co-author for *Chicken Soup for the Soul*. She has written many books and articles on parenting, including multiples, which have been inspired by her four sons.

Over the years, Susan has worn several hats. In addition to her freelance career, she worked as a Senior Editor for a publishing company. Later, she honed her marketing skills by promoting literacy and programs at a public library system. Currently, she utilizes her passion for writing and education as a Communications Coordinator for Kansas State University.

A native of Michigan and graduate of Michigan State University, Susan loves her adopted home in Florida, where her kids were born and raised. In her spare time, she reads anything she can get her hands on, snuggles her two cats, assembles jigsaw puzzles, and thanks God for her blessings.

You can reach Susan through her website at www.susanheim.com.

Karen Talcott is the co-author of four *Chicken Soup for the Soul* devotionals books, for Women, Mothers, Tough Times and Wives. Several of her stories have also appeared in other *Chicken Soup for the Soul* books. When inspiration strikes, she likes to sit down at her computer with the window open for fresh air and let the story idea take over. She is thankful for her husband and three children for being supportive of her writing.

Karen resides in South Florida and finds her best time to seek God's wisdom is on morning walks with her beloved Golden Retriever.

Story ideas and titles seem to flow as she communes in God's world. In her spare time, she enjoys all moments with her children, cheering on her favorite SEC football team (Go, Dawgs!), and volunteering with struggling readers in a local elementary school. Whether you are picking up this book for yourself or giving it as a gift, she hopes you find that the heartfelt devotions are an uplifting reminder of God's constant and enduring love.

Thank You

We appreciate all of our wonderful family members and friends, who continue to inspire and teach us on our life's journey. We have been blessed beyond measure with their constant love and support.

We owe huge thanks to all of our contributors. We know that you pour your hearts and souls into the stories that you share with us, and ultimately with each other. We appreciate your willingness to open up your lives to other Chicken Soup for the Soul readers.

We would like to thank Amy Newmark, our Publisher, for her generous spirit, creative vision, and expert editing. We're also grateful to D'ette Corona, our Associate Publisher, who seamlessly manages twenty to thirty projects at a time while keeping all of us focused and on schedule. And we'd like to express our gratitude to Barbara LoMonaco, Chicken Soup for the Soul's Webmaster and Editor, and Chicken Soup for the Soul Editor Kristiana Pastir, for her assistance with the final manuscript and proofreading. And yes, there will always be typos anyway, so please feel free to let us know about them at webmaster@chickensoupforthesoul.com, and we will correct them in future printings.

The whole publishing team deserves a hand, including our Vice President of Production Victor Cataldo, and our graphic designer Daniel Zaccari, who turned our manuscript into this beautiful, inspirational book.

Sharing Happiness, Inspiration, and Hope

Real people sharing real stories, every day, all over the world. In 2007, *USA Today* named *Chicken Soup for the Soul* one of the five most memorable books in the last quarter-century. With over 110 million books sold to date in the U.S. and Canada alone, more than 300 titles in print, and translations into nearly fifty languages, "chicken soup for the soul®" is one of the world's best-known phrases.

Today, thirty-one years after we first began sharing happiness, inspiration and hope through our books, we continue to delight our readers with ten to twelve new titles each year but have also evolved beyond the bookshelves with super premium pet food, a podcast, adult coloring books, and licensed products that include word-search puzzle books and books for babies and preschoolers. We are busy "changing your life one story at a time®." Thanks for reading.

Share with Us

We have all had Chicken Soup for the Soul moments in our lives. If you would like to share your story, go to chickensoup.com and click on Books and then Submit Your Story. You will find our writing guidelines there, along with a list of topics we're working on.

You may be able to help another reader and become a published author at the same time! Some of our past contributors have even launched writing and speaking careers from the publication of their stories in our books.

We only accept story submissions via our website. They are no longer accepted via postal mail or fax. And they are not accepted via e-mail.

To contact us regarding other matters, please send an e-mail to webmaster@chickensoupforthesoul.com, or write us at:

Chicken Soup for the Soul
P.O. Box 700
Cos Cob, CT 06807-0700

One more note from your friends at Chicken Soup for the Soul: Occasionally, we receive an unsolicited book manuscript from one of our readers, and we would like to respectfully inform you that we do not accept unsolicited manuscripts, and we must discard the ones that are sent to us.

Chicken Soup for the Soul.

Miracles, Angels & Messages from Heaven

Amy Newmark

Paperback: 978-1-61159-116-3

eBook: 978-1-61159-351-8

More inspiration, hope, and faith

Chicken Soup for the Soul.

Angels
and the
Miraculous

101 Inspirational Stories of Faith, Miracles and Answered Prayers

Amy Newmark

Paperback: 978-1-61159-104-0
eBook: 978-1-61159-341-9

for your reading pleasure

Chicken Soup
for the *Soul.*

Devotional Stories for Women

101 Devotions with Scripture, Real-life Stories & Custom Prayers

Susan M. Heim & Karen Talcott
foreword by **Jennifer Sands**

Hardcover: 978-1-61159-084-5
eBook: 978-1-61159-145-3

More devotions to help you find

Chicken Soup for the Soul

Devotional Stories for Mothers and Grandmothers

101 Devotions with Scripture, Real-Life Stories & Custom Prayers

Susan M. Heim & Karen Talcott
foreword by Lisa Whelchel

Hardcover: 978-1-61159-096-8
eBook: 978-1-61159-134-7

inspiration, peace and happiness

Changing your world one story at a time ®
www.chickensoup.com